Leading
Instructional Rounds
in Education

A FACILITATOR'S GUIDE

THOMAS FOWLER-FINN

HARVARD EDUCATION PRESS
CAMBRIDGE, MASSACHUSETTS

Library of Congress Control Number 2013931903

Paperback ISBN 978-1-61250-526-8
Library Edition ISBN 978-1-61250-527-5

Published by Harvard Education Press,
an imprint of the Harvard Education Publishing Group

Harvard Education Press
8 Story Street
Cambridge, MA 02138

Cover Design: Erin FitzPatrick
The typefaces used in this book are Minion Pro, Myriad Pro, and Fenice.

CONTENTS

FOREWORD

Instructional rounds is a countercultural practice. It asks educators to learn new ways of thinking and acting at multiple levels. In classrooms, it challenges the assumptions many have by focusing on the instructional core—on how students and teachers are interacting in the presence of content. It brings together educators—frequently teachers and administrators, who don't normally collaborate—into networks where they are observing side by side, describing what they see in nonjudgmental language, and then carefully forming patterns and predictions and brainstorming next steps. It pushes people to move away from the isolated norms of idiosyncratic practice to look at systems of improvement and make coherent connections between classroom, school, and district improvement strategies. Rounds requires educators to unlearn old patterns and collaboratively learn new ones.

This all takes an enormous amount of adult learning. Facilitators play critical roles in creating and sustaining network cultures that support the learning needed to make deep change in cultures and practices. When they start rounds work, many facilitators see themselves as managing the more technical aspects of it: helping schools develop problems of practice; ensuring that the participants stay in the descriptive voice as they take and report their observation notes; guiding them through analysis and pattern-making, predictions, and the next level of work. But facilitators quickly find that rounds is not just a packaged program. Facilitators need to be building network skill and understanding, constantly assessing where the group is and what it needs, acting as skilled teachers of adults, and figuring out what the next targeted learning should be. It is hard, challenging, messy, and critical work, and it is often lonely work, with little clear, written support on how to be a good facilitator.

Enter Tom Fowler-Finn.

Tom Fowler-Finn was school superintendent for five years in Cambridge, Massachusetts. I knew that Tom had worked with members of the Harvard team (Richard Elmore and his colleagues Elizabeth City, and Sarah Fiarman, from the Harvard Graduate School of Education and authors of *Instructional Rounds in*

Education) to bring instructional rounds into the Cambridge public schools. However, it wasn't until I was halfway around the world in the tiny town of Colac, in Victoria, Australia, that I came to appreciate him as a rounds facilitator.

I had been invited by the network leaders of the Barwon South Western region to go on school visits with them, observing their rounds practice, and sharing my own experiences. It was a great learning journey for me, leading six rounds visits in six days in cities, towns, and tiny rural schools along the southern coast of Australia. In our debrief of the third visit, one of the network leaders, Jan Rollinson, suggested a different way to facilitate the discussion of the next level of work. It was a nifty structure that tied the next level of work discussion back into the instructional core and focused the visiting groups in ways that provided for a much deeper discussion about improvement suggestions for the school. Always happy to learn new ways to improve the rounds practice, I asked Jan to lead that part of the protocol the next day. When she did, I thanked her and asked her where she figured that out.

"Oh," she said, "I learned it from Tom Fowler-Finn. There was a workshop on rounds in Gippsland that he was leading, and my network sent me there a few months ago. He was full of good ideas." So that was my first, but not my last, opportunity to learn something important about rounds from Tom Fowler-Finn.

After seeing some significant gains in student learning from the rounds work in Cambridge, Tom took to rounds facilitation when he retired, and he took to it seriously. In the last few years, Tom has probably facilitated, and taught facilitation, in more settings than anyone else in the world, working not just in the United States, but also as *the* go-to rounds trainer and facilitator in Australia. Tom took to rounds work with the intensity, curiosity, and careful data-driven approach that he brings to all his work. With a keen eye for experimentation and an unremitting focus on the instructional core, Tom has developed a thoughtful practice as a facilitator.

In this book, Tom shares the results of those years of work. *Leading Instructional Rounds in Education* is a detailed facilitator's guide to a thoughtful and well-honed version of the rounds practice. It is very much Tom's way of doing it. Taking a close look at the original instructional rounds model, Tom has drawn on his own background and carefully documented learning processes, added his own improvements, and codified the process in concise and direct language. Tom minces no words as he outlines what facilitators should do and should not do, how to predict where the rounds practice may go off the rails and become unproductive, and what to do about it. If you are looking for a clear how-to guide to facilitate a disciplined and well-thought-out version of instructional rounds, this is it.

In facilitating instructional rounds, there is a natural tension between experimentation (to bring in new learning and new approaches) and structured teaching and learning of the practice (to ensure fidelity to the model). Every facilitator will approach rounds in his or her own way. While in my own practice I tend toward the more open-ended side of the spectrum, many aspects of my facilitation practice resonate strongly with the goals and practices Tom outlines in the book, and a number of things I have learned from reading it have pushed my thinking. Among the many aspects that stand out for me in this book:

- *Ties to inquiry and outside knowledge:* The book keeps a tight focus on making improvements in the instructional core and specifically on raising the cognitive demands on students. Tom explains in detail what improvement may look like for teachers, students, and task (see chapter 3), and throughout the book, he weaves in outside sources (like materials from the National Council of Teachers of Mathematics) to remind us that educators' observations need to be informed by, grounded in, and connected to outside research on instructional improvement. He urges facilitators to model this commitment as they plan and implement professional development for their networks.
- *Precision of teaching the practice:* Tom has a very clear idea of what the network participants need to know and be able do, and he offers a variety of precise "lesson plans" for supporting the participants' learning. During the previsit training, when the participants watch videos to learn how to observe, for example, he suggests stopping the video every few minutes to check for understanding and to share sample observations. He emphasizes the use of benchmarks to help participants rank and compare the quality of problems of practice, pattern statements, predictions, and suggestions, prizing precision and usefulness to the host as his standard.
- *An emphasis that rounds not start or end with just the visit:* The book makes clear that the facilitator role starts well before the visit and lasts for months afterward. Tom offers specific protocols for sharing follow-up work and acknowledges the changes in culture needed if educators are to give advice to their peers. He includes plans in chapter 5 for private follow-up implementation talks with local school leaders at the end of a visit and in chapter

8 for setting clear expectations that local school leaders will make substantive efforts to resolve their problem of practice.

- *A facilitator stance that advocates learning:* The book speaks directly to would-be facilitators, helping them negotiate entry, set ground rules, and know what is important and what should be nonnegotiable. Embedded in Tom's advice to facilitators is the belief that learning and implementing this process precisely takes time and lots of it. Facilitators need to make sure busy school people carve out enough time to do it properly, or not do it at all. Tom also applies this learning stance to the work of the facilitator as well, modeling this approach and urging other facilitators to continually tune their practice, using year-end and visit-end forms to capture feedback from participants.

Leading Instructional Rounds in Education makes clear how critical facilitators are to helping adults learn their way into new approaches, behaviors, understandings, and ways to work with one another.

Recent research on the developmental arc of rounds work in districts underscores this. When my colleagues and I, along with other members of our rounds team, conducted research on a sampling of districts with four or more years of rounds practice, we discovered that for some, rounds was primarily an "event"—something that happened on a given day at a given school. Some educators we talked to in these settings were quite positive about the ways the visits were opening up classroom practice, sharing ideas across schools, and helping to develop a common language and understanding about teaching and learning among the participants. Others felt stuck, frustrated about not getting the deeper changes in large-scale instructional improvement that they sensed were possible. Still others believed they had progressed past the sticking points.

When schools and districts realize that the work is not about "doing rounds" but about instructional and organizational improvement—that it is less about what happens at a visit than what happens before and after it and that it needs to be tied to clear improvement strategies and explicit plans for adult learning—the countercultural changes become even deeper, and the demands on the facilitators ratchet up even higher.

As the practice moves beyond the technical demands of organizing a visit, facilitators have to do much more than just learn and put into place a set of protocols and procedures. They need to know more than the *how* of rounds. They must understand the *why*, so they can best apply, tune, and customize the rounds practice to the local setting, while keeping in mind the larger prize of instructional improvement at scale. All the practices for deeper impact—planning visit follow-up, calibrating the learning of the network and the school, connecting to larger school and district improvement strategies—require deeper cultural change and place more of a leadership and cognitive burden on the facilitator. Last month, I was sharing some of these connections between rounds and deeper improvement work with a group of facilitators in Michigan. One of them raised her hand, cleared her throat, and somewhat hesitantly spoke up. "I have been facilitating rounds for almost two years now," she said. "I always saw my role as the keeper of the protocols. Now I see it is much more."

It is much more. This is new, challenging, and vital work for rounds facilitators. Supporting them as they help us change our schools into places that routinely and deliberately support the learning of all children is essential. This book provides a valuable resource for facilitators as they embark on this important journey.

Lee Teitel
Lecturer on Education
Harvard Graduate School of Education,
and coauthor, Instructional Rounds in Education

Introduction

Instructional rounds is being embraced today by school districts across the United States and around the world. While the idea of using classroom observation to improve instruction is not exactly new, the finer points of this approach to school improvement are.

The process of instructional rounds was developed by Harvard Graduate School of Education professor Richard Elmore and his colleagues Elizabeth City, Sarah Fiarman, and Lee Teitel, as described in *Instructional Rounds in Education: A Network Approach to Improving Teaching and Learning* (Harvard Education Press, 2009). The authors based the idea on the professional practice of medical rounds used by doctors in teaching hospitals. Medical rounds is a teaching and learning process by which attending doctors lead groups of residents and specialists to patients' bedsides to interview, observe, and analyze the available medical data, before they develop a plan together for treatment. As a tool for the teaching and learning of new doctors in the shared culture and practice of medicine, and as a method of institutional self-improvement, medical rounds has long served the profession well.

This is the idea instructional rounds has borrowed to help districts self-improve. Networks of educators gather specific, nonjudgmental classroom observations on school self-identified problems of student learning to make and implement recommendations for large-scale improvement.

Instructional rounds attempts to bring rigor to school improvement, not by blaming teachers, but by focusing on the learning of top-to-bottom leadership, the folks most able to effect change. It does this by bringing school and district leaders—teacher leaders as well as union heads, principals, district level leaders, and superintendents—together into the classroom to take a close look at teaching and learning. It creates a way for them to work together to understand what aspects of the instructional core need fixing and then how to make this change happen across classrooms, schools, and districts—at scale. The process offers a far more ambitious and hopeful approach to learning improvement than approaches that focus on one teacher or even one school at a time.

Instructional rounds is essentially about adult learning. It raises questions about the professional culture and practice of educators at all levels of a school system, forcing conversation about how we, as educators, can ask students to do critical thinking when we rarely apply it to ourselves. By helping us figure out and describe what good teaching and learning look like, instructional rounds helps us uncover ways that we can support each other to get there.

As a systemic improvement strategy, instructional rounds is a seemingly simple idea that is subtle, yet deceptively complex to put into practice. As a form of shared inquiry, instructional rounds may be difficult to understand at first, but once integrated into practice, it can be transformative. Essential to this transformation is the thoughtful support and firm guidance of a skilled facilitator to make sure network members develop the necessary culture and practice that lead to real improvement. As an experienced facilitator, but also as someone who has worked with instructional rounds in a variety of roles, I offer this book in the hope that it will provide those charged with leading instructional rounds the support and guidance they will need to facilitate with knowledge and confidence.

MY FIRST EXPERIENCE WITH INSTRUCTIONAL ROUNDS

I was first exposed to instructional rounds when I was serving as superintendent of schools in Cambridge, Massachusetts. At the time, the district was burdened by multiple problems and was spending well above the state per-pupil average while achieving well below the state average in student test scores. Our district needed to think about how to improve teaching and learning in broadly systemic ways. At this time, I was attending monthly superintendent roundtables led by our neighbors at the Harvard Graduate School of Education. Elmore and his colleagues were focused on finding ways to help educators develop the same kinds of critical thinking skills and conceptual understanding we were hoping to instill in our students. Concerned about school leaders who knew they had problems with teaching and learning but didn't know what to do about it, Elmore was looking at how to get them the training, skills, and knowledge they needed for figuring out what was not working and fixing it. He was exploring an early iteration of instructional rounds as a way to improve adult learning through building a community of practice—a way to collaborate around looking at what was happening within the instructional core of teacher, student, and content for clues about how to do better at engaging all students with challenging content.

Building a Network

After one of these meetings, I asked him about creating a Cambridge School District team of central office educators and school principals to investigate how we could come together as a leadership group to engage in a shared understanding of effective teaching and learning to improve student outcomes. We both understood that skilled facilitation would be critical to the success of this work. This led us to launching the Cambridge Leadership Network, which was composed of principals from each of our fifteen schools, some central office staff, the high school's deans of instruction, Paul Toner as president of the teachers union, and me as superintendent. All of us were led by Elmore and his colleagues, City and Fiarman—about thirty people in all. Our mission was to do whatever it took to improve student learning. As my first experience with instructional rounds, the work was compelling, fascinating, and thrilling.

We began by learning about the critical instructional core, namely, the interaction of teacher and student in the presence of content—an interaction that gets played out in the work that students do—and went on to relearn how to observe in classrooms to be objectively descriptive and to examine and analyze what we saw. We were soon on our way to developing a practice for understanding what was happening in the classrooms, but still had not yet sufficiently connected the work of our school data teams to daily practice in ways that could help us improve. We began to target critical questions of student learning in order to engage in more purposeful classroom observation as a way to define problems of practice. This helped us better understand the cause-and-effect relationships between our professional practice and student learning. In light of what we learned, we as a school district reconsidered, reconceived, and restructured our organization and our professional lives.

Moving from Rounds to Implementation

Our rounds work changed our school improvement planning. The network members benefitted from what we had learned in each other's schools as we transformed a collection of competing schools fighting for financial resources into a school district collectively responsible for the learning of all students. We began budgeting on the basis of improving student learning across the system instead of competing for per-school allocations. As a school district, we became more transparent in all that we did by virtue of a shared network language and a culture of increased respect among colleagues.

We completed seven rounds per year, and it was not until the second year that we realized how much we had changed individually and as a network. The Harvard team, as we called them, guided and nurtured our development by creating activities that pushed us to learn more about what was taking place in our schools and to rethink what we were doing. The team raised questions for which we had no immediate answers. These questions, however, helped shape our agenda for network learning through our rounds work. Our facilitators' support, enthusiasm, and confidence in our progress led us to eventually own the work and continue it even after our formal relationship with the Harvard team ended. The first two years of external facilitation from the Harvard team were followed by two more years of internal facilitation from our deputy superintendent of schools, Carolyn Turk, and various cofacilitators. In addition to being a rounds participant during that time, I was focused as superintendent on directing the restructuring of the school system to improve learning at scale. This experience gave me a deep understanding of how a superintendent benefits from rounds participation and can predicate organizational decisions on what has been learned through this process.

Facilitating

I now work as a full-time facilitator, consulting for districts across the United States and Australia. In this capacity, I find my background as teacher, curriculum leader, and superintendent invaluable in giving me access to the many points of view that different educational positions bring to the process.

This book shares what I have learned about this work. As a guide for facilitators, it draws on Richard Elmore and coauthors' original seminal work, *Instructional Rounds in Education* (henceforth referred to as *Instructional Rounds*). My approach has been honed by my own experience facilitating instructional rounds and training facilitators. While each facilitator finds ways to make the practice his or her own, and skilled facilitators may vary in their approaches, my goal here is to present the tools and practices that have been helpful to me in the hope that you will find them equally useful.

My book presupposes familiarity with *Instructional Rounds* and cannot be properly understood without it. Nevertheless, I will give a nickel tour of the subject before focusing on what facilitators in particular need to know.

WHAT IS INSTRUCTIONAL ROUNDS?

Instructional rounds is a collegial, network-based approach to improving teaching and learning; this approach, based on observations in the classroom, results in recommendations for improved student learning. The process is not complete until network-generated recommendations for improvement are acted upon by school and network members.

Rounds is premised upon the proposition that high-quality teaching and learning district-wide can be produced only through the coordinated support and shared responsibility of a committed collegial leadership network. In doing the hard work of educational improvement through questioning their current practice and changing their professional culture, networks need help, support, and guidance; they need a facilitator.

Implemented at its best, rounds leads to systemic improvement of teaching and learning through the creation of a shared-network culture. This culture, developed through the increased knowledge and shared practice of distributed leadership (leadership that includes all relevant academic players, from teacher leaders, assistant principals, principals, district-wide curriculum or instruction directors to superintendents), is the first step toward improving learning at scale.

Rounds Is Developmental

The development of a shared culture and language to improve student learning, as well as learning to share responsibility for implementing what is learned through rounds, takes long-term commitment. Participants may only require several rounds of school visits to gain basic command of the process and develop the method's technical skills—classroom observation, evidence gathering, analysis, debriefing, and creating recommendations. Developing a shared culture and practice, on the other hand, takes much longer. Acquiring both technical skills and a shared practice require rethinking one's professional practice and making commitments that extend beyond the rounds sessions into all areas of decision making and professional life.

As a facilitator, you will need to guide the development of skills, a network culture, and a shared practice, while continually challenging the network members to press forward. You will need to help the network develop and maintain norms, develop trust in you and the other members, own the work, and form a binding commitment to take collective responsibility for what is learned in the classroom. This commitment must be enduring, for it is likely to take three to four years before network learning and action find their way into broad-scale, lasting institutional change.

Rounds Is Complicated

Network members initially find it confusing and difficult to apply new concepts and unfamiliar language to teaching and learning. Having to continuously question and rethink their practice is exhausting. There are many steps to the rounds process, and members find it quite complicated before they understand how each step builds upon the prior one. Members find it intellectually demanding to be asked to sort out patterns of observation without judging. A facilitator plays an important role in helping members make sense of what they are seeing in the classroom.

Rounds Is Messy

The work is replete with unexpected events and seemingly contradictory developments. Events go off schedule, participants need more time, network-developed norms are sometimes ignored, protocols are misinterpreted, and discussions get derailed. As facilitator, you will be more successful by allowing network understanding to muddle along at its own pace, while insisting at the same time on strict rules of objectivity and honesty.

The work can generate difficult emotions in members asked to think critically about their day-to-day work practice. Many may feel defensive, even embarrassed, about work they once thought was fine. Members are going to need your support as they struggle to leave behind old professional habits, just as they will rely on your help in the face of work that can be messy, complicated, and confusing. You are their guide through these challenges, and in this, protocols are your friend.

A BRIEF OVERVIEW OF THE BOOK

This step-by-step guide will explain the aims of facilitation at every stage of the work, address questions and points of confusion experienced by facilitators and network members, and offer advice on how to become a skilled rounds facilitator of a productive network. It will discuss the facilitator's role and job functions, outline protocols and activities for conducting rounds sessions, provide support and presentation materials, and, finally, detail instruments useful for assessing network progress.

This book is intended for educators of all levels interested in what is involved in facilitating instructional rounds networks. The chapters are introduced in the same chronological sequence that a facilitator would use to conduct a rounds session for a newly formed network. They can broadly be divided into four sections:

1. Anchoring facilitation
2. Pre-rounds work
3. Facilitating school rounds visits
4. Implementing the work

Anchoring Facilitation

Chapter 1 explains what you need to consider in meeting with a district hiring authority before signing on to the job. If you do sign on, there is much you need to know about your role and the job functions. Key among these is the kind of network you will be working with. I describe some of the key concepts of effective facilitation.

Pre-rounds Work

Chapter 2 helps facilitators to convene a first meeting with a host school in preparation for a rounds visit. An agenda for the host school meeting is provided, as well as a model classroom visit schedule and tips on helping the host school develop a problem of practice to guide the rounds visit work.

Chapters 3 and 4 discuss the network training session. Included are a template for a letter of introduction and an invitation to this first network meeting as well as an agenda for this two-day in-service. The two chapters cover the day-long exercises and the background theory behind many of these activities. The details within these chapters should provide most of the tools facilitators need to gain the confidence to eventually make the work their own.

Facilitating School Rounds Visits

Chapter 5 begins with directions and materials for facilitating a school rounds visit, including an agenda and a description of your role and duties during this on-site visit. Chapters 6 through 8 detail the specific process and protocols for analyzing the observational notes collected during the classroom visits and developing the next level of work.

Implementing the Work

Chapter 9 provides guidance on a facilitator's ongoing work to promote school improvement and professional change after these rounds visits have ended. This is when the real work of implementation and improving student outcomes begins. The facilitator's job is to help network members think through how this work connects to school and district-wide outcomes, as well as how to overcome obstacles to change.

A FINAL WORD

Much of the material for this book comes from my work over the past years facilitating rounds across the United States and Australia. I have worked with single schools, small school districts in New England, medium-sized to large school districts from California to New Jersey, and very large regional systems in Australia. This book benefits from what I have learned from literally thousands of feedback submissions solicited from participants on both continents at all points in the process to understand what help they found most useful. I have also learned much in following these same districts over time. The work of facilitating rounds is challenging and requires a sense of urgency coupled with confidence in the process and a belief in network learning. It demands flexibility and agility. Some of the most important aspects of the work of a facilitator involves being alert and responsive to network needs in its role as a force for change.

When I began work as a facilitator, it was before *Instructional Rounds* was written. I remember being relieved and grateful at how freely the Harvard team shared their documents, presentations, and other material. Instructional rounds as a method for school improvement can be powerfully effective. For this reason, Elmore and his colleagues would like to see its ideas shared as much as possible. I have the same intent. This book is designed as a next iteration, a kind of road map, of the work.

In this spirit, the book is focused on the work of the guide, the facilitator. While any network member might find it helpful, it is written with the facilitator in mind. I have tried to clearly define the facilitator's role and job functions at every stage of the work, attempted to anticipate the potential questions and points of confusion often experienced by network members (and facilitators), and aimed to be as helpful as possible by including support material, presentation samples, procedural protocols, activities for conducting sessions activities, and assessment instruments for evaluating the network's progress.

Facilitating in rural, suburban, and urban settings with varying degrees of school autonomy and district administrative structures has broadened my perspective and helped me to distill my own practice. I have learned much about what makes effective facilitation by guiding some thirty on-site facilitators and cofacilitating with many. A number of times, I wished I could have begun the work by handing them some kind of how-to book to help them assist others to supplement with what they may have already learned from *Instructional Rounds*. This book is a result of that desire. I hope you find it useful.

PART 1

Anchoring Facilitation

CHAPTER 1

Networks and the Facilitator's Role

You are about to embark on a challenging, but exciting journey. It's going to be long and hard, but it's all for a good and important cause: large-scale improvement of student learning. As the facilitator of instructional rounds, you are the guide on this journey, and your only tool at the moment is this book and the knowledge and experience in your head. Your challenge ahead is enormous: to ask a group of often midcareer educational leaders to make themselves vulnerable—to open themselves up to self-scrutiny and change. You will be teaching them serious technical skills for this journey, but the adaptive skills they'll need to change the way they work and the way they conceive of their jobs, their colleagues, and themselves—the cultural changes needed—is by far the hardest part of the trip.

Fortunately there are guideposts for this journey in the form of protocols to follow for developing the skills they'll need, as well as the cultural norms they'll be writing to help themselves learn how to work together as a team. But most importantly, they'll have you—their guide, their facilitator. They will need you fiercely at first, and then, as they become more skilled and adept, they should eventually mature into a self-governing force for change. This is when you will know you have done your job well.

But first, let's start at the beginning, when it's just you and your crew: facilitator and network. Let's talk about how you come together.

THE BEGINNING

As districts vary, so do networks. Networks come in various shapes and sizes, but nearly all of them reflect the districts they serve. This chapter discusses the different kinds of networks; how their size and member composition reflect different purposes; how they are conceived of by a convening authority (often a superintendent); and how their structure can sometimes be a prediction of success or failure.

With all this variability, so can the role of facilitator also change, depending upon whether the facilitator is a district insider or hired as an outside consultant. This chapter also discusses the various roles of the facilitator.

In this chapter, I describe the first things you need to discuss when you are hired. There are a number of important issues to clarify with the convening authority, your boss, before you sign on to the work. For example, a facilitator needs to understand what it means to be selected from within the district versus coming in as an outside consultant; how this impacts the job responsibilities and work; and what the separate roles of cofacilitators might be. Later in the chapter, I will examine how rounds work is designed to wean networks from dependence on facilitators and how a network and the facilitator's role can affect the productivity of the work.

Please note that despite the multiplicity of facilitating circumstances and the differences between varying districts, networks, and facilitator combinations, the protocols and actual work of instructional rounds itself remain constant.

NETWORKS AND DISTRICTS

When a district's leadership (usually the superintendent or assistant superintendent) asks a facilitator to lead a rounds process, the first conversation should be about why the leaders are interested in rounds work. The facilitator should discuss the leaders' areas of concern in the classroom and what they hope to achieve. (See exhibit 1.1 for a list of questions a facilitator will need to discuss.)

Committing to instructional rounds is a serious investment. Districts should understand the resources required. District personnel who agree to serve as members of the rounds network should know they will be asked to commit a minimum of 1½ days per month in rounds meetings alone. Then there's the possible cost of their substitute replacements, the need to ensure that school leaders have coverage in place while they're away from their office or school, the meeting and clerical costs, and the cost of facilitation. This huge commitment should be considered carefully by district leadership. These matters can present logistical and financial challenges to school districts of all sizes.

Networks As a Reflection of a District's Purpose

Once a district has committed to making the large-scale, long-term investment that is instructional rounds, a facilitator's next important issue of discussion is the

---

EXHIBIT 1.1

Facilitator Checklist: Questions for Convening Authority

- Purpose for doing instructional rounds?
- To whom will the facilitator report?
- Will the superintendent participate?
- Will cofacilitation (or facilitators in training) be included in the design?
- How will network membership be determined?
- How many schools will be visited over what period of time?
- How will host schools be determined?
- What will be the duration of the launch and rounds sessions?
- How much time will be allocated for the facilitator(s) position?
- Who will follow up on implementation of the next level of work?
- Will the members be expected to write a theory of action, and will this be incorporated into district operations?
- Will the schedule allow for convening interim meetings of the network?
- Will a think tank be established to help guide the work?
- What kind of clerical support will be provided?

---

creation and composition of network membership. Network groups comprise different constituencies, depending on purpose and resources. Membership may vary from the large-district (or multiple-district) representation of superintendents and central office administrators pressing for large-scale regional change, to the more single-minded focus of a principal and lead teachers from one school. Some networks have more of a community focus and may include outside stakeholders like prominent citizens or involved parents, in addition to school district staff. Other networks may be somewhat more academic and include education professors or other academic professionals.

The composition of a network makes a statement about the culture of the district and how it regards the challenges of implementing what is learned through rounds. A network composed by choice of only central office staff is more likely to represent a controlling, top-down culture of leadership seeking compliance. This is usually not about staff buy-in and lasting change. Other times, it's a sign that district leadership little values input from school building staff, a position antithetical to building a shared culture and practice. In tightly controlled networks composed of only central office staff, trust in the organization is often low and rounds is not likely to result in change. Facilitators should beware of closed networks like these.

At the other end of the spectrum, networks that lack central office personnel and are composed solely of staff from a single school face huge odds against accomplishing lasting change. They will be hampered, if not defeated, in reaching their goals without district support on matters such as staffing, curriculum, district assessments, pacing guides, and in-service programs.

The greatest potential for positive change is found in *district-wide networks*: networks that represent a single district and whose membership includes a superintendent, central office staff (from curriculum to special education), school-level administrators, teacher leaders, and teacher union representatives. (District-wide networks nonetheless have their own special problems, with staff nervous about criticizing one another—problems I will detail further on.)

How to Create Networks

As a first order of business, facilitators should discuss what student learning the district or other convening authority hopes to gain from rounds. This is an important conversation that will have a big impact on how far the work carries into the organization. Facilitators are a unique resource to assist district leadership to think through this vision.

Once a vision of what the convening authority hopes to gain has been understood, the facilitator should explore what positions and individuals should be represented in the network. Those most connected with accomplishing the identified learning improvement are obvious candidates for network membership. Implementing educational improvement at scale is necessarily a shared practice that requires shared responsibility. If a district hopes to achieve district-wide change, network membership must include a wide range of positions, from school-level to district-level leadership, including the head of the teachers union.

Forcing participation is never a good idea in selecting network members and is unlikely to help the district achieve its purpose; rounds work requires proceeding with an open mind. A few skeptics can be one thing, but more than a few makes it difficult to develop the shared practice and culture of an effective network. Such resistance interferes with network learning. A school district unable to field the appropriate number of willing members is not ready to begin rounds. Facilitators need to confront this issue with district leadership before agreeing to facilitate (a conversation that can be uncomfortable particularly for in-house facilitators).

Composition of a Network

District-wide networks should include representatives from the full range of grade levels—pre-K to high school. A culture of shared leadership means feeling responsible for all students, from the time they enter school to the time they leave. There's much to be learned about a student's full school experience, which happens by conducting rounds at all grade levels. Involving all grade-level leadership means doing away with the isolated leadership roles of the past that compartmentalized grade levels and learning. A culture and practice founded on a shared responsibility for all students means including all grade levels. Privatization and isolation of practice cannot achieve learning at scale.

Inclusion of New Staff in Networks

I am often asked whether new staff members should be included in networks. Membership in the network is a great way to matriculate into a new position. There is no better way to form bonds and learn about how the organization functions than to take part in the evolution of district culture and practice.

Districts That Hope to Expand Their Number of Networks

When large districts intend to increase their number of networks over time, the inaugural facilitator(s) will need to anticipate managing such an expansion. You do this by selecting several initial network members for their potential facilitating skills and then create dedicated cofacilitator-in-training positions during that first year. The positions get replenished from within as trainees gain the confidence and facilitation skills necessary to run a network. The two new facilitators can be paired for support as they assume the facilitation of the same network, while you, the mentor, move on to initiate a new network, thereby replicating the training cycle.

Network Size

Every network is different, from large, fifty-person groups to small, twelve-member groups. Networks may have narrowly focused missions or have broad, multi-pronged agendas; their members perhaps represent low-income urban school districts or well-funded suburban schools; or they may represent single schools with small student populations or multiple school districts with thousands of students over vast geographical areas. (Geography can also be a factor in determining a network membership. In some of my Australian districts, for example, it took more than four hours to travel from one end of the district to another.)

Groups of twelve are rather small. If the network is ideally to include all the positions necessary to effect comprehensive district change, then a twelve-member network is unlikely to include the full range of positions, from central office to school leadership, necessary to establish the agency of the network within the district. Regardless of membership size, it helps to include multiple principals and teacher leaders for them to feel sufficiently comfortable to speak openly.

Networks are generally too big when they have more than thirty-six members or more than eight teams. The authors of *Instructional Rounds* and I have worked with networks of forty to fifty people, but I strongly recommend against it, because of the number and size of the observation teams that descend into schools and classrooms. Networks larger than ten teams or forty people are better established as two separate networks. These two networks can be joined at different points, such as for the launch session, and then separated for school rounds visits and brought back together for special interim sessions of reflection and in-service throughout the year. These are called *helix networks*.

Truly large districts are best served by multiple networks, which can be run simultaneously while growing incrementally. New Jersey's 23,000-student Elizabeth Public School District, for example, increased its number of networks over three years. The networks' initial launch session was composed of members from the district's senior leadership, including a few principals, while subsequent networks focused on broadening membership to include all principals, assistant principals, and teacher leaders. The district used interim meetings to unite these separate networks. It now has six ongoing networks, with more anticipated.

District-Wide Networks

Whether the district is large or small, single-district networks (district-wide networks) provide opportunities to accelerate improvement at scale because the collegiality among network participants yields a potent shared culture. Once the participants have clarified common goals, they can form and coordinate a shared practice across the district, providing each other with the feedback needed to focus progress.

(As a small bonus, school visits can be a delight when colleagues and students up and down the grade levels encounter each other in the hallways. I recall students at one middle school calling out in excitement to see former principals and teachers from their elementary school.)

The only caveat is that sometimes, the civility of the personal bonds within district-wide networks creates a very strong culture of nice that can impede the kind of tough, honest communication needed to get the work done. Staff members can also feel more nervous about being observed by people they know well, while facilitators hired from within the district may find it challenging to take on a leadership role with their colleagues. Generally speaking, members of district-wide networks feel acutely accountable to their colleagues in host schools and so accept special responsibility to produce agonizingly well-substantiated work. They tend toward obsessive reviews of evidence to ensure that it is well vetted, that patterns are painstakingly substantiated, and that work is as thoughtfully worded as possible. This leads to network processes that take much longer to complete. Members may feel that all too much is at stake, including their own reputations. These fears along with the culture of nice are likely to prove intractable for several rounds or more.

I recall one network so concerned about the impact of objective evidence on the host staff, its members tried to use the predictions phase of rounds to reassure the principal, while coming up with good things they believed staff would like to hear. The trouble was that their predictions had no basis in evidence. In another case, a network member proposed to end the rounds session with a host school's list of positives. Appropriately, someone pointed out that rounds does not yield positives and negatives, but instead aims for objective pictures.

Facilitators must be alert to this and remain firm in asking members to stay focused and on course. An effective facilitator expresses confidence that the staff can learn from objective feedback and use it productively to solve student learning problems.

FACILITATORS

Clarifying District Commitment

To gain the robust improvement for which instructional rounds is designed, facilitators must have district support from the get-go—facilitators can't move forward without the full backing of the district. Facilitation is a serious time commitment. Before signing onto the job, you must make sure that at a minimum, the district understands the amount of time required to facilitate. This is a long-term commitment and generally at least a quarter-time position from the perspective of an in-district person. Facilitation is more than an add-on job and should be recognized as such. Duties include, besides the 1½-day rounds sessions themselves, ongoing occasional meetings with the district, meetings between rounds with host schools, regular meetings with your advisory network council or the think tank (explained later in this chapter), preparation for the in-service launch session, prep time before and after each session, and follow-up, including ongoing school and network support for implementation of what has been learned from rounds. All facilitators should be wary if a district authority does not allot them sufficient time. Expectations on all sides will be unrealistic and unlikely to be met.

Whether an internal appointment or external selection, facilitators need to meet with host schools, with special attention to the first host, to help them develop a problem of practice (often involving a bit of in-service instruction before the first meeting of the network). The network's training comes in the form of a two-day in-service through the launch session, which is scheduled before the first school visit takes place. Every rounds visit includes an hour or so of additional in-service on topics such as the role of members as small-team facilitators, building common understanding of terms such as student engagement, or analyzing school data to develop a problem of practice. Meeting arrangements and other clerical work can be done by others, but also require facilitator coordination and oversight.

The preceding descriptions illustrate some of the time commitment and resources necessary to implement rounds—commitments that must be established up front. Accordingly, facilitators either appointed from within the district or brought in as an outside consultant should plan for this kind of time in their personal schedules.

In the long term, instructional rounds is a developmental process that requires a minimum of three to four 1½-day school rounds visits, held once per month, before participants have confident command of the process. District-wide networks should conduct a minimum of four rounds visits annually, with additional interim visits for in-service and reflection maybe twice a year. It then takes two to three years before members fully understand how to implement this learning and before results begin to show in classrooms. Often, a district's enthusiasm for a rounds approach to improve learning results in a decision to begin the work without taking into full account the sizable time and resources required.

Think Tanks

Continuity of planning for rounds visits and postvisit reflection is built into the process through the creation of a kind of guidance council called a think tank.

Think tanks are important to the work of the network and should reflect the network's makeup, with members coming from a variety of grade levels and a central office position or two. The members should include individuals willing to express concerns or praise and able to clearly analyze what is taking place. They help plan network agendas, offer insight and feedback, and can be important to the growing independence of the network over time. I find it helpful to meet with think tank members to discuss their sense of how the agenda is working and how the network is progressing. The more networks take responsibility for their operation and work, the more productive they become.

The facilitator recruits volunteers for this work, while the convening authority who knows the network individuals better will decide which think tank members may best provide critical leadership for the network over the long run. One of the facilitator's early conversations with the convening authority (often superintendent or assistant superintendent) is to discuss the functioning roles of a think tank. (Superintendents have too much power within the district and probably shouldn't sit in on the think tank.) The think tank is not actually recruited and selected until after the launch session. During the launch session, a facilitator asks for volunteers to serve on an ad hoc think tank for the purposes of conducting business during that launch session. This gives members a chance to assess whether they'd like to take part in actual ongoing think tank work. It is not until the end of the launch session that the facilitator seeks volunteers for the extended work of the think tank over the remainder of the year.

Reporting to the Hiring Authority

Generally, a facilitator reports to a district superintendent. A consultant–client relationship with district superintendents requires formal, periodic check-ins, even when the superintendent is a member of the network. These private meetings are generally strategic, with the initial discussion focusing on defining the network's purpose and follow-ups serving as progress reports. This relationship with the superintendent may be in addition to whomever the facilitator regularly reports to coordinate activities and develop improvement strategies. Sometimes, meetings are necessary to address problems within the network itself, for example, with a group that is having trouble implementing what it has learned.

Network members must trust that what they personally confide to the facilitator will not be revealed when the facilitator meets with the superintendent, just as a district leader must feel the facilitator is presenting a frank, accurate, and insightful picture of network progress.

The superintendent's perceived interest in the work and respect for the facilitator's role are important public indicators of the district's commitment to change. Developing organizational culture and practice are the superintendent's purview, and if the superintendent does not invest the time, then the district's commitment to the work falls into question.

Even when the superintendent is highly committed, there can be problems arising from his or her relationship with school boards, which are notoriously impatient for results. Justification for tying up costly resources is often in the background of school board questions. Feeling this kind of pressure, superintendents may believe they need to get as much out of instructional rounds as possible in as short a time as possible.

As a former superintendent of schools, I deeply understand this sense of urgency. But it doesn't necessarily mean you will have to fight for the time necessary to put into practice what is learned through the work. In fact, this same sense of urgency can result in increased backing from a superintendent hoping to expedite the process. It can be a potent relationship when support for implementation strategies is jointly planned between facilitator and superintendent. Quantifiable improvements through test scores are never immediate; so facilitators can be of help backing the superintendent by explaining to the board why the time necessary to see results will be years as opposed to months. Meanwhile, the superintendent might find ways to clear the path for implementing changes that arise out of rounds. Rounds work, unfortunately, requires a large commitment of time and money, particularly in the first year. Sometimes, superintendents are reluctant participants in rounds work—work their leadership team may deeply value. This can cost them influence within the organization. Sometimes, these two leadership forces work at cross-purposes when networks try to accelerate implementation while a superintendent is occupied with pressing matters elsewhere.

This happened when I was consulting for the Australian regional director in the Gippsland district of 150 schools. Over the first year, in my position as facilitator, I periodically met with the director and frequently met with the assistant director in charge of rounds work. The director, a talented leader with a difficult and demanding job, was supportive of our work, but struggled to commit much time, because she was otherwise engaged. During our second year, however, as her educational team began talking more and more about the instructional core, using a common language of terms she didn't know, and proposing organizational changes based upon a developing culture unfamiliar to her, she cleared her schedule to join the work. In a remarkable demonstration of shared learning and practice, she joined our network as an equal and then prominently, enthusiastically, and knowledgably took part in the work, incorporating it into her job and leading the district to accelerated progress. It is very hard to get the work done without buy-in from the person at the top.

Internal Versus External Facilitators

The working role of the facilitator is a bit different, depending on whether he or she comes from inside or outside the system or functions as part of a team of paired internal and external cofacilitators (or even paired in-house cofacilitators). The many strengths and weaknesses of each kind of leadership are fairly obvious: in-house candidates know the district well, but are vulnerable to insider politics. Entrenched relationships can burden forward movement. External consultants, on the other hand, are more immune to district politics and more likely to be perceived as experts, but are less familiar with the inner workings of the district. Districts are probably best served by cofacilitators, because they offer the best of both worlds—someone from within the district and a consultant from outside. Cofacilitators can be appointed as mentor-trainees, with the outside consultant in the lead, and the in-house candidates projected to assume leadership when the network is ready to carry the work forward on its own. The reason to choose one form of rounds facilitator over another very much depends on the district's purpose and, of course, the limits of district resources.

Internal Facilitators and In-House Politics

Institutions are designed to endure, which generally makes them allergic to change and instinctively bent on defeating reformers, especially in-house reformers. An organization's power structure makes it easy to marginalize even those tasked to effect positive change. This is why internal facilitators can face steep challenges when facing the power hierarchy of school governance alone. I once heard school leaders refer dismissively to their colleague and network facilitator as just "someone who does rounds."

Another time, I worked with a talented facilitator whose inside position as a staff developer made it difficult for her to push a reluctant principal of a host school too hard. She came to me in my role as critical friend to report that the principal seemed unwilling to share the results of network findings after an observational visit to his school. She said she had not only talked with the principal about moving forward, but also volunteered to help him do so. After trying a number of different tactics, she never succeeded in getting the principal on board. The result was a considerable waste of school staff time and effort, not to mention that of the network.

It is not uncommon for principals to want to shelve a presentation that could upset faculty. Discussing network results with faculty is always difficult. Anticipating this, the facilitator and other network members can offer support to help principals present this material to the faculty. The structure of the rounds session can help in this regard. Implementation progress reports from host school principals are a standing agenda item, and network members eagerly await hearing how their observations have been received by host school faculty.

The necessity for host school follow-through may be something to raise with your think tank members. The case of the staff developer appointed as a facilitator is one that would obviously have benefited from bringing in an outside consultant to work as cofacilitator to help drive institutional change.

The Independence of Outside Facilitators

External facilitators are generally much less hesitant to take on organizational culture. Improving learning at scale is uncomfortable work for administrators, and many must be supported, tutored, coaxed, or sometimes pushed into making change. This is not to say that a facilitator can move forward without consulting the district leader, but skilled external facilitators often have the independence and experience needed to work through the discomfort caused by change. Even external facilitators, though, can find it challenging to fly solo. They miss out on opportunities provided by cofacilitation to discuss and reflect upon the unique issues of leadership, to brainstorm solutions to issues that arise, and to benefit from team analysis of sensitive personnel dynamics.

Cofacilitating

The combination of internal and external strengths works well together. Internal facilitators are familiar with the people involved in the district organization. External facilitators are usually more experienced with rounds and with the challenge of reorganizing school systems to take advantage of what is learned through rounds. This knowledge may mean a more confident and fresh point of view untangled by job relationships and the inherent organizational culture. Consultants can diplomatically voice what insiders can't. I have heard more than one internal facilitator say, "Well, you can say that because you don't work here," or, "I could never get away with saying what you just said."

The training of cofacilitators drawn from inside a network is an incremental process. Many trainees appreciate support that allows them to begin with small steps in ways that feel comfortable to them. At first, a trainee may wish to watch and take notes on what the facilitator does, helping with group work initiated by the facilitator. The next step would be to take on a portion of facilitation work—perhaps leading a group at making predictions or devising the next level of work. Most learning is in the doing. The facilitator trainer should always make time for a debrief at the close of each session the trainees lead. As they move into full cofacilitation work, the facilitator can move into a side role providing support as a critical friend.

The Facilitator's Role Outside the Group

As facilitator for the network, you have a definite and particular position that stands in many ways outside the group. You must be constantly mindful of how your role is different from that of a member of the network proper—a distinction that both you and the participants must understand. Your job is to guide the network members to work together as they struggle to interpret what is happening in the classroom in terms of a specific problem of teaching and learning. In this way, it is not merely your role to focus more on the network process than on the content of their work (which is what they own and you help them achieve); it is your job to ensure that they function as a collaborative community of leaders and work together to accomplish their student learning improvement goals.

The Facilitator's Role in Leading Inquiry

Rounds is an inquiry-based process, meaning a facilitator raises questions and presses the team to find answers. Rounds facilitation is in large part one of scaffolding, or assisting participant thinking by asking thought-provoking questions that preserve task complexity and cognitive demand (Mary Kay Stein et al., *Implementing Standards-Based Mathematics Instruction: A Casebook for Professional Development*, 2nd ed. [Reston, VA: National Council of Teachers of Mathematics, Teachers College Press, 2009]). You are not there to provide answers, specify what should happen, or demonstrate how best to accomplish the team's aims. Facilitating is not like coaching; it is more Socratic, more a way of challenging the participants to develop the depth of understanding they will need to observe and analyze that which is central to their work, the classroom's instructional core. As they struggle to understand the reasons for objective, nonjudgmental observation, for example—as they attempt to connect the concepts to the practice—they will be visibly frustrated.

Be careful about stepping in. Providing examples may help illustrate the concepts, but skillful facilitation helps people make the connections themselves.

The Facilitator's Role As a Rational Voice

Network members will need you to be dispassionate in helping them become untangled from side issues that arise during the inevitably passionate discourse of debate. Your role is never to take a position in these debates—a role that poses special challenges if you are working within your own district. You must monitor discussions without expressing an opinion, as well as live with the results of the outcome. You will need to function more as referee in insisting on discussions that stick to evidence, stay on track, honor multiple perspectives, consider all relevant information, and remain impersonal.

Grouping Within the Network

All of the actual work that takes place during a rounds session involves teamwork. Creating groupings for these teams matters, as does who is responsible for creating the groupings. The options for grouping members within rounds sessions are many. Facilitators design the structure and numbers of groups, but it is the convening authority, perhaps an assistant superintendent, who knows the individual members and who should be in charge of assigning names of members to the facilitator-designed team organization. The composition of each small group should represent the characteristics of the larger school network and include perspectives from different grade and leadership levels.

When these individual teams are joined as pairs and form medium-sized groups for the analytical work of discerning patterns of evidence from classroom observations, making predictions, and generating options for improvement, membership in these larger, midsized groups benefit if they include representation from the central office, school building leadership, and teacher leaders. This is because a range of organizational viewpoints yields more insightful debriefing and more comprehensive recommendations for the next level of work that take into account the shared responsibility of all involved in lasting change.

It helps to develop a long-range plan to ensure that every network member has a chance to work with every other member of the network in small or midsized teams. Experience has shown that working closely together during rounds leads to higher mutual professional regard. Planned grouping increases the sharing of a professional culture and practice that improves network and organizational functioning. This means reassigning members to different teams at every new rounds session. For this reason, group assignments are best not made by individual host school principals because the history of prior groupings of the entire network is difficult to track and planned interaction of all members over time is an especially onerous job for the host principal, who must prepare the classroom visit schedule, the practicalities of the visit, and the development of the problem of practice with the staff.

Network members occasionally make special grouping requests that need to be honored throughout the life of the network. In one large network, two sets of spouses requested to be separated, and in another, an individual felt unable to work with another person for long-standing, personal reasons. The groups were accordingly adjusted. More rarely would a facilitator need to change team members midway through a session, though it is sometimes done for special network purposes or to stimulate new lines of thought.

Other grouping options, of course, are possible, ranging from random to special-interest and job-similar groups. When it comes time to write a theory of action, network members with similar jobs may benefit from working on their documents together.

Balancing Network and Observation Team Size

In terms of team size, smaller observation teams of three to four (no more than five) people are best. Teams of five or six members in the same classroom are imposing and more likely to ask the same students the same questions, whereas smaller teams are more easily accommodated especially in crowded classrooms, or classes with small enrollments.

Initial debriefing of observations seems to work well for teams of three to six members, but teams are combined, doubling their number, during the later stages of debriefing and the next level of work. For this reason, a network's number of teams is always even because teams are paired for much of the postobservation work. When teams of five to six then grow to midsized teams of ten to twelve, equal participation and productivity suffer.

In larger groups, members sometimes engage in side conversations, individuals can feel enough anonymity to give up on participating, while others get lost struggling to read the team's data. Richard Hackman addresses the issue of effective team size in *Leading Teams* (2002):

> So what is the best group size? It depends on the task, of course, but I do have a rule of thumb that I relentlessly enforce for student projects in my Harvard courses: A team cannot have more than six members. Even a six-person team has fifteen pair

[possibilities] among members, but a seven-person team has twenty-one, and the difference in how well groups of the two sizes operate is noticeable.

The research Hackman cites on the relationship between group size and productivity indicates that teams in the range of three to six members take the best advantage of the diverse contributions of the collective while still remaining efficient. Bigger teams show a decline in productivity per person.

Using a guideline of three to four members per observation team yields more productive midsized teams of six to eight people at the most. If there are thirty-two network members, the school should plan for eight teams visiting four classrooms each. The size of each team does not always work out, but the goal is to err on the low side of team numbers, given what can happen with larger, midsized teams. Members do sometimes miss sessions at the last minute, so if some teams are listed at five, attrition may take care of the problem.

Improving Your Practice

However your job is framed, you will develop your own way of facilitating. As you gain experience, you will see opportunities to do the work differently each time. You will need flexibility in your responses to each network's unique challenges. A facilitator's practice is always changing—through feedback from network members during and after every rounds visit, from session feedback forms, from brainstorming sessions between rounds sessions with network leadership, from working with new networks, and through trial and error. All forms of debriefing are valuable: from cofacilitators, from fellow consultants, and from follow-up visits to previous host schools.

FINAL THOUGHTS

You want to work with districts committed to change. If you sense that the district is interested in doing rounds but doesn't recognize that the work should lead to all-encompassing, organizational, and system-wide change, then the work is unlikely to succeed. Sometimes you'll run into district leaders who think you're just talking about teaching and classroom change. These leaders need to understand that rounds work leads to structural change such as modifications to budget, personnel, and leadership practices, as well as instructional and curriculum alterations, not to mention adjustments to other district institutional systems and maybe even to how the superintendent conducts business. Facilitators fundamentally need to know what kind of commitment and investment the district expects to make—not just in the process, but also in the implementation of network results.

Instructional rounds requires a personal commitment from all the members to act upon what is learned through rounds and to declare their intent to implement what they've learned, by writing a theory of action—a map for enacting the network members' vision of organizational change. If writing a theory of action isn't understood by district leadership and guaranteed up front, a facilitator should question whether the district is serious about making the changes necessary to improve learning. A theory of action requires a district authority (superintendent or designee) to publicly back systems of accountability that show up throughout decision making. In authorizing instructional rounds, district authorities guarantee that members will receive the in-service and support necessary to follow through on what has been learned through rounds. In turn, members (teacher leaders, the assistant superintendent, principals, curriculum leaders, and the superintendent) agree to follow through on their theories of action. These documents explicitly state what the participants are going to do to improve learning.

The first question you may hear from members is whether everyone writes theories of action, who reads them, and how they will be used. Even though participants will not be asked to write a theory of action until they have significant rounds experience, all members should understand they'll be expected to demonstrate this personal commitment when they join the network.

Importantly, this expectation and the accountability system of follow-up is something that must come from district leadership rather than a facilitator. A facilitator's job instead is to assist members in writing effective theories as part of their focus on supporting implementation efforts.

It is best to work out answers to questions of commitment to change with the superintendent before you sign on for the work. If the support and resources aren't there, change won't happen, and your work as a facilitator is unlikely to make much difference. At some point as a prospective facilitator, you may need to decide whether the work can succeed, depending on what you hear from the convening authority. You should anticipant that some districts just aren't ready to do rounds, and you should be able to recognize this when it occurs. Otherwise, it becomes a Sisyphean task—painful and frustrating for all involved.

Commitment to using theories of action comes from the district and reflects the determination of the district's leaders to improve learning, knowing that this means changing culture and practice. I was pleased to hear a New Jersey school superintendent acknowledge just this when he said: "Your theory of action defines you as a leader." Pablo Munoz, superintendent of the Elizabeth Public School District in New Jersey, then added then he'd be happy to share with the network his and the school board's theory of action, saying he considered them "public documents." It is one thing to do rounds, and quite another to commit to a plan of action based upon what is learned from rounds. The doing doesn't result in much, he said; it is the acting upon that makes a difference.

PART 2

Preparing for Instructional Rounds

CHAPTER 2

The Pre-Rounds Host School Meeting

T his chapter describes how facilitators prepare schools to host rounds visits. Facilitators need to meet privately with a host school's leadership team well in advance of the network's rounds visit to make sure the school understands the purpose of the visit, the protocols to be followed, what the network members will be looking at in the classroom, and what small, but nontrivial logistics need arranging.

The most important agenda item, however, is to help each school settle upon a problem of practice. A problem of practice is a school-identified problem with student learning that could be improved if the school knew more about the problem and what action to take. A problem of practice helps focus network observations during their classroom visits.

The initial, pre-rounds host school meeting is a bit different from all other host school visits in that it takes place before the network's launch session (detailed in the following chapter) and therefore before anyone at this school has been trained in rounds work. For this reason, a facilitator's visit to the first host school involves giving that school's leadership a bit more in-service rounds training than the other host schools. Otherwise, the pattern for subsequent pre-rounds visits to host schools is pretty much the same.

SELECTING HOST SCHOOLS

When you become a facilitator for a district new to rounds, one of the first things you discuss with the superintendent, assistant superintendent, or other convening authority is the district's area or areas of concern. Second, you need to agree upon the first host school. All schools should be encouraged to be host schools, but not all should go first. For the first host school, the superintendent should choose a school in which the principal is trying to move her or his school forward, is anxious for objective feedback, and is able to face the challenge. It helps if the school has already targeted learning problems that can serve as a solid and straightforward problem of practice, since this school will be used to introduce the network to rounds work.

Host schools need to understand what instructional rounds will ask of them. The first thing facilitators need to make clear to potential host schools is the time and resource commitments this work entails.

Additionally, host principals should understand the importance of involving faculty and staff in rounds work from the very start. This begins by having members of the school leadership, including key relevant personnel such as teacher leaders, deans or curriculum heads, attend your initial meeting with the principal. Their work will continue all the way through to the implementation of rounds recommendations. This key group is known as the internal rounds leadership team.

Even though high-performing schools benefit from rounds work (showing that rounds is more than just an intervention for struggling schools), they are not always the best choice for the initial host (especially if their high scores can be attributed to the intellectual capital of their students). Students from advantaged home environments often learn regardless of a school's teaching and learning practice. High-performing schools can certainly still identify and develop worthwhile problems of practice, but only if the school is truly interested in receiving network help. For schools at the top, the question is whether the staff believes that rounds is about more than showing off the good work already taking place.

Likewise for low-performing schools or those with significant achievement gaps, the question is whether their staff believe student learning problems are actionable by staff. Do the staff members attribute learning problems to the kind of students they receive or the kind of teaching they do? Are they willing to look at teaching and learning from the perspective of what students make, do, say, or write in the classroom as the best predictor of performance? Staff efforts to close achievement gaps should consider the importance of improving student engagement.

Good candidates for the initial host school are those schools that (a) have a clear understanding that student learning at their school needs to be improved and (b) have a staff eager to publicly acknowledge and address the school's learning problems.

CONTACTING THE HOST SCHOOLS

When facilitators first contact host school principals to set up a pre-rounds host school meeting, they will want to discuss which student learning problems at the school could form a basis for the school's problem of practice and network observations. Facilitators might ask whether learning problems have already been identified through faculty work, perhaps as part of school improvement planning. Regardless, they'll need to suggest that the principal have a broader discussion with the faculty about the network's visit. This faculty meeting should discuss what problem of practice they consider most important to advance student learning, as well as what is of greatest interest to faculty and staff.

The reason for asking whether faculty has had input into an area for network focus is because this influences how network findings are received. If faculty have taken part, the facilitator should be interested in their viewpoint. If faculty won't be involved, the facilitator needs to know why not, and whether there is a plan to involve them. A disconnect between the problem of practice and faculty investment in creating it will limit faculty commitment to solutions and could short-circuit follow-up action. Early faculty involvement is the difference between a faculty that feels acted upon by a rounds visit and one that feels it is taking charge of improving student learning.

THE MEETING AGENDA

For pre-rounds host school meetings, you should always go to the school. You need to tour the facility, and your visit is a way of acknowledging the school staff's control over the process. The pre-rounds meeting with the host school is designed to take care of a number of things: reassure nervous school staff, offer a crash course on instructional rounds, and help them hone their problem of practice. All schools must articulate their problem of practice well in advance of the network's visit. This is most demanding, as noted, for the first host school because it occurs before this school has been taught how. But this is what your visit is partly about—to help the school identify and clarify a particular problem with student learning. (Problems of practice will be further explained later in the chapter.)

The learning goals for the visit include making sure the host school understands that rounds visits are about network professional development, school learning, and large-scale student improvement—not about evaluating teachers or judging the school (exhibit 2.1). Make sure that the school understands the expectations for behavior by students, staff, and especially the network during the upcoming rounds visit. The facilitator will need to schedule the date for the network's rounds visit, discuss the particulars of the rounds day's schedule, ask the host school to draft a classroom visit schedule, and, finally, tour the facility to make sure adequate

---

EXHIBIT 2.1

The Pre-Rounds Host School Meeting

Goals for the Meeting

- The host school will understand the purpose for instructional rounds, as well as what will take place on the day of the visit.
- Behavior expectations for staff, students, and network are clearly understood.
- Host school staff will draft a problem of practice.
- Host school staff will leave the meeting with all questions answered.

Agenda

3:00 Introductions. Discussion of school and network interest in instructional rounds.

3:15 Discussion of rounds process, network norms, and visit protocols. Develop a problem of practice out of school context and data.

4:00 Describe how the school should create the classroom visit schedule. Clarify the approval process necessary for modifications to the schedule and the problem of practice. Help principal prepare remarks to be made on the morning of the rounds visit.

4:15 Tour facility, particularly meeting space, and review arrangements for the visit—parking, technology, etc.

4:30 Adjourn.

---

private space and other essentials can be secured. These pre-rounds meetings generally run about 1½ hours.

WHO ATTENDS THE MEETING

Facilitators should encourage principals to have the school's leadership team members at these meetings to serve as an internal rounds leadership team so that they understand the purpose and function of the work. This puts into practice the shared-practice principles of rounds culture and school improvement. The assistant principal, teacher leaders, instructional coaches, and school's union representative are unlikely to all be a part of the network, but at the principal's discretion, they are good candidates for the internal rounds leadership team to work with the principal in implementing rounds work. This meeting is a time for them to ask questions and weigh in on matters.

Regard inclusion of union representatives in networks and school leadership teams as an asset. It certainly helped in Cambridge for the teachers association president, Paul Toner, to be a member of our network. Not only was he an active and thoughtful participant, but his participation accelerated our work. By giving teachers who feared a network visit an accurate insider's account of the rounds process, he was able to reassure them. This helped get us off to a good start. Toner eventually became president of the Massachusetts Teachers Association and a strong supporter of instructional rounds as an effective method for improving professional practice and student learning.

DISCUSSING THE UPCOMING ROUNDS VISIT

Most schools are nervous about the scrutiny, especially since faculty usually associate observational visits with evaluation. During a discussion of the norms of the network and visit protocols, they will need reassurance that they can trust the professionalism of their colleagues to remain true to the rounds' mission of non-judgmental observation based on a question raised by the school. Address this up front by inviting candid discussion when you thank the school for volunteering to be a learning lab for the professional development of network members. You can acknowledge and attempt to assuage their fears by further emphasizing the confidential nature of the work. One of the first significant messages a facilitator needs to convey is that while the content of specific classroom observations must be kept confidential within the network, the process and outcomes should be transparent and endorsed by all. It is incumbent upon the host school to inform its entire staff about what to expect during these visits and what protocols members will follow. Schools need to hear exactly what to expect when the network comes calling: how the classroom visits proceed, how long they last (twenty minutes each), whether teachers should or should not prepare (no), and how observers can be expected to behave in the classroom. Teachers need to be told that they shouldn't stop class to introduce network observers and that the observers will be sensitive not to interrupt lessons. It should be clear to teachers before the rooms are visited that members come and go in silence without introductions, and so on. Teachers may wish to place chairs in their rooms as a starting point for visitors but with the knowledge that the visitors will, when appropriate, walk around the room to talk with students and observe their work. Teachers are not sure what to think about hosting a rounds visit, so host schools are expected to have a pre-rounds discussion with faculty before the network arrives.

Finally, you should inform the host school that if all goes as planned, the principal and leadership team should have printed copies of network findings the next day after the visit. Principals typically share with staff these observation results soon after the rounds visit.

THE PROBLEM OF OVERPREPARATION

In some cases, schools prepare weeks in advance for the network's rounds visit. Staff and faculty pore over the classroom visit schedule, sometimes meeting after hours to coordinate lesson plans for the day.

These schools have clearly misunderstood the nature of rounds, which is to observe teaching and learning in the classroom around a particular problem. Ironically, however, the role of the teacher and student as learner is the most important and the least impacted by advance lesson planning. Established roles take a long time to change. For teachers to prepare atypical lessons, though, can muddy the observation data and prevent the school from obtaining information about typical student learning experiences—information that could help the school improve.

If the school's leadership seems to be misunderstanding what is being discussed in this initial pre-rounds meeting, facilitators should offer to return to meet with the host principal and the entire faculty prior to the actual rounds visit to clarify the theory behind the rounds process and then further detail what the faculty can expect during a rounds visit. It is very important to emphasize again at this time that the purpose of the visit is not teacher evaluation. An open faculty meeting with voluntary attendance to discuss rounds can reduce anxiety and create better understanding.

A last note: if network rounds visits were to gain a wide reputation as a process that requires significant advance planning, this could discourage other schools to volunteer as hosts. If rounds as a nonevaluative process designed to help schools improve is publicly misunderstood across the district as instead an evaluation instrument or a demonstration effort, this misapprehension might demand considerable effort to correct.

THE PRACTICALITIES OF THE ROUNDS VISIT

As a facilitator, you must be very familiar with the practicalities of the rounds visit and be able to explain these details to the host school. Details that seem clear in theory may become confusing when put into practice. For this reason, it is important to work with the host school during this pre-rounds meeting to hammer out the details of the rounds sessions.

Establishing the Rounds Classroom Visit Schedule

You will need to have the school's leadership draw up a classroom schedule that details each team's four classroom assignments. As a facilitator, you should bring along a sample rounds visit schedule for discussion and illustration. You will need to explicitly state how many teams will be visiting and how they are to be paired. Visit schedules can vary, depending on the needs of the school. Occasionally, schools request that the network focus tightly on a few classrooms or require the visitors to give a glimpse into as many classrooms as possible. Both of these approaches work well in service of a productive problem of practice. For the purposes of this book, I will focus on the approach typically used in setting up classroom visits, in which four teams visit four classrooms. (See exhibit 2.2 for a sample schedule.) Note that the instructions on the bottom of the schedule detail precise protocols for how the classroom visits need to be arranged. Although the sample schedule shown in exhibit 2.2 does not show the problem of practice that will be the basis for classroom observations, this information is normally included on the schedule as well.

Typically, classes are visited multiple times. Classrooms selected for a visit should reflect typical teaching and learning circumstances in the school, and all grades should be visited. That is, unless the problem of practice focuses on particular subject areas like math or science, for example, or on a particular range of grade levels. In such cases, the schedule should be developed accordingly. This may require alteration of teaching schedules to coincide with network observation times. Altering teaching schedules sometimes creates undesirable difficulties. In one instance, one of our elementary schools had a problem of practice around writing. All teachers altered their schedules and lessons in all content areas accordingly to include writing work in every class. Halfway through the observations, it became obvious that the students' hands were getting tired.

Setting up the schedule is not simple, since it involves ensuring that pairs of teams visit the same classroom at different times. It may involve intricate work

---

EXHIBIT 2.2

Rounds Classroom Visit Schedule

Teams and Team Members

Group 1	Group 2	Group 3	Group 4	Group 5	Group 6
Ann	Michael	Alvin	Shana	Ian D	Marcus
Nate	Simon	Sean	Petunia	Maribel	Delphos
Tao	Lily	Kyla	Jason B	Cecil	James
George	Marvin		June	Miguel	

Classroom Visit Schedule

	Group 1	Group 2	Group 3	Group 4	Group 5	Group 6
8:15–9:00			Network meeting			
9:00–9:20	Rm 4-G.1	Rm 12-G.3	Rm K1-G.K	Rm 7-G.3	Rm 20-G.6	Rm 11-G.3
9:20–9:40	Rm 12-G.3	Rm 4-G.1	Rm 7-G.3	Rm K1-G.K	Rm 11-G.3	Rm 20-G.6
9:40–10:00	Rm 18-G.5	Rm 16-G.4	Rm 22-G.6	Rm 17-G.5	Rm 2-G.1	Rm 5-G.2
10:00–10:20	Rm 16-G.4	Rm 18-G.5	Rm 17-G.5	Rm 22-G.6	Rm 5-G.2	Rm 2-G.1

This is a typical instructional rounds visit schedule printed by the host for the network on the day of the rounds visit. A total of twelve different classrooms will be observed, with every group visiting a full range of grade levels. The number of groups may be increased to eight or ten (always even numbers), in which case four or eight additional classrooms would need to be added to the schedule. In the case of small schools or visits limited to portions of a school, some classrooms may need to be repeated more than others to create a full schedule. Please notice how Groups 1 and 2 have the same four classrooms in common, as is true for Groups 3 and 4, and Groups 5 and 6.

to complete the schedule in such a way that each pair of teams, Groups 1 and 2 and Groups 3 and 4, say, observe the same four classrooms but at different times. Members gain a more complete and objective view for understanding classroom teaching and learning when paired teams pool their data in debriefing. Evidence gathering is much enriched when there are different perspectives from different teams that have visited the same room but at different times. In this way, for example, one team will see the beginning of a lesson, and the other team will see it completed.

I am often asked why the members visit only four classrooms. I have discovered that a four-classroom schedule yields as much worthwhile observation data and captures practice as well as a five-classroom schedule does. The time that might be spent on visiting a fifth classroom cuts back on valuable additional time that is better used for debriefing.

Network members develop a deeper understanding of a school's practice if they are able to observe all grades and subjects, or as many as they can, across the school. This brings a broader swath of the school's practice and student development through the grades to the members' work when they consider all observation evidence in rounds debriefings.

Once questions on scheduling are addressed, facilitators leave the work of creating the schedule to the host school, but ask that a copy be sent for the facilitator to review a couple of days prior to the visit. Host schools are usually happy to know that the schedules will be checked to confirm that all is in good shape.

Which Teachers Should Expect to Be Visited by the Network

In describing the rounds visit to the principal, the facilitator makes it clear that all teachers should be willing to participate. For principals to seek specific volunteers for observation contradicts a belief in open and honest professional discourse. It is a core tenant of rounds philosophy that private practice is no longer acceptable. Furthermore, if a schedule is based only on volunteers, it is unlikely to yield observations representative of the full student experience at that school. This is counter to the rounds emphasis on making teaching and learning visible through a focus on the practice, not the person.

When anxiety is high and a principal fears negative reactions among teachers required to participate, the facilitator might suggest that the principal invite teachers who wish to be excluded to see the principal in private. A private discussion of their concerns, along with explanations about the aims of instructional rounds, usually alleviates the problem. In my years of rounds, I have seen very few teachers ask to be excluded out of anxiety—a request that can be accommodated if absolutely necessary. There are good reasons for exceptions, such as for a planned field trip, certain self-contained special education classrooms, or a classroom scheduled for testing. In these cases, schedules can be adjusted.

Sometimes, host schools provide teachers with the visit schedule ahead of time. I recommend against this. One or more teachers may be unexpectedly absent the day of the visit, and the network will want to change the schedule to avoid visits to classes taught by substitutes. Teachers expecting to be observed tend to become stressed when the visit schedule is not followed. If, for some reason, the visit schedule is distributed, the names of network members should be omitted because the work is independent of the person; no one should focus on who is doing what, and team assignments can change because of absences or other factors. I advise providing schedules to network members only, with all teachers put on notice that they are likely to be visited.

THE PRACTICALITIES OF THE HOST'S BUILDING

Since all schools vary in their physical facilities, you must make sure that the host school has planned for private, secure, and adequate space for the day with the required technology. The important work of rounds should not be wasted simply because the members of the network had no room to interact with each other, couldn't spread out and analyze the observation data, or had inadequate space to display their work for review and revision.

Physical Facilities Checklist

A building tour checklist should include a large, private room for network meetings; a computer with electronic projection equipment for PowerPoint presentations; enough tables for flexible groupings as well as a separate table for the facilitator; a steady flow of coffee and tea; and adequate logistics for snacks, lunch, and so forth.

Rounds meetings are often held in libraries or cafeterias because of the table and display space required. Wherever the session is held, the room must be absolutely private for confidential discussion and secure for material displays. If it is held in a school library, the in-house school staff will be unable to access the library and library workroom space for the entire day.

Lunch is often eaten in the same space that the network meeting is held. Going out is a poor option because time is tight. Often you can ask a school to arrange for catered sandwiches. In most cases, districts make sure that host schools are not obliged to finance lunch or pay for any other incidentals.

The second day, which concludes before lunch, is best held where there is adequate parking and lots of room, especially confidential space away from the host school. Occupying the host school's library for another day is restrictive to school activities. At an off-site location, even if it's another school, the host school network members will find themselves less distracted and all the network members will feel freer to converse openly.

Aides or Secretarial Help

Making the practical arrangements for rounds can be time-consuming in the beginning. Many districts prepare "rounds carts" that can be transported from one host school to the next. Boxes of supplies for each team—pens, notepaper, sticky notes, poster paper, and the like—should be replenished in advance of each rounds session so that each meeting and visit is ready to go without much trouble.

Hopefully, a facilitator has coordinated with a district secretary who is dedicated to accompany the network on all visits to manage the distribution of supplies throughout the day and to produce network work products such as patterns, predictions, and the next level of work as they are created. Facilitators benefit greatly from this kind of assistance, which enables them to focus on the opening presentation and ongoing network dynamics. Working with the same secretary for the duration of the year provides continuity of knowledgeable assistance in a myriad of ways, including the documentation of session work in established formats. This documentation in predictable formats is helpful for reference when reflecting on the growth of the network and when, or if, host schools are revisited in a year or two. Consistent documentation enables a ready comparison to track school changes.

DEVELOPING THE PROBLEM OF PRACTICE

A problem of practice refers to an unresolved question or dilemma of student learning. It focuses on one element of practice. It involves shared inquiry. This is often a problem the school may have identified as important in the school improvement plans. A problem of practice serves as the focus for the network during a rounds visit. It is stated as a question about student learning—a question that would improve student outcomes if addressed.

Developing a problem of practice for network focus can be challenging. Nearly all principals and leadership teams will require a facilitator's help with this. Once rounds is under way, a facilitator can bring along samples from prior host schools as models. Student learning problems can usually be found in data the schools already have or in the work they are already trying to do. A problem of practice needs to be designed as a specific inquiry about student learning and must be definable, observable, and actionable by the school. *Instructional Rounds* describes a productive problem of practice as having the characteristics listed in exhibit 2.3.

It is the host school's job to identify the student learning problems of greatest concern, while the facilitator's job is to help the school hone a problem of practice out of what will be of the greatest value to the school's improvement efforts as well as to network development.

Assisting, Rather Than Leading

As a facilitator, you want to be sensitive in describing your role as assisting rather than leading the school's administrative team in crafting these problems. For school leaders, taking the lead in devising their problem of practice themselves can give them a reassuring sense of control over the process. Besides helping with the technical side of the process, a more supportive and less aggressive facilitating role communicates that the network's goal is to improve rather than judge—clarifying to the school that it will be respected and can trust the process. This approach means that when the rounds process is finished, the network will have gathered a large amount of unattributed and valuable observation data that will be analyzed for information pertinent to the school's stated inquiry. Thus, in helping schools design a problem of practice, facilitators are helping them make a formal request to the network for detailed information and insight about the staff's chosen learning problem so that school staff can make informed decisions about what to do next.

Where to Find a Problem of Practice

The school likely has the makings of a problem of practice within its assessment data, school improvement plans, or professional development efforts. Although the situation should really be the reverse: productive school improvement plans

---

EXHIBIT 2.3

Characteristics and Guiding Questions for a
Productive Problem of Practice

Characteristic	Guiding Questions
The problem of practice (POP) focuses on the instructional core.	Can you visualize what you would like to see happening in the three areas of the instructional core (teacher, student, content) if this POP is successfully addressed? Is it clear what model teaching and learning would look like?
The POP is directly observable.	Is it possible to gather observation data in the classroom that addresses the POP? What kind of observation data can be collected to address the POP in such a way as to enable further learning and school or network action?
The POP is actionable.	Is the question raised in the POP one that is within the power of the school to control, modify, or improve? Is the action necessary to respond to the question within the responsibility and power of the school staff to address in a reasonable amount of time?
The POP connects to a broader strategy.	Is the POP connected to a school improvement strategy or to an area of study by the network? Is the POP supported by other evidence in quantitative and qualitative data? Is the POP applicable to multiple grade levels and classrooms and to all students in those areas?
The POP is high leverage.	If the POP is acted upon productively, would the actions result in a significant difference in student learning? Could these actions become a model for further application throughout the school? Does the POP address an issue of strategic educational importance to the school or network?

Source: Adapted from Elizabeth A. City, Richard F. Elmore, Sarah E. Fiarman, and Lee Teitel, *Instructional Rounds in Education: A Network Approach to Improving Teaching and Learning* (Cambridge, MA: Harvard Education Press, 2009).

should be based on problems of practice, regardless of whether the school is engaged in rounds work or not.

A school improvement plan might focus on any number of areas, such as students taking responsibility for their learning or the extent to which students are engaged in critical thinking skills. Both examples could serve as the basis for a problem of practice. Analysis of data pulled from low state math scores, for example, might help staff to zero in on a particular problem of practice. See exhibit 2.4 for some examples of problems of practice.

Challenges to Problems of Practice

Sometimes, even though schools have prepared a problem of practice for early network review, they occasionally decide on something the members of the rounds network know little about. In these situations, I often hear anxious concerns from members who fear they won't be able to adequately observe.

This happened when I was working with an elementary school in New Jersey that was hoping for insight into engaging students in math talk. Knowing nothing about math talk, many participants felt too unprepared to go forward. But early identification of the problem of practice gave me enough time to give them advance reading on the topic and arrange a short in-service session at the end of the prior school's rounds session (when I often take time for a short in-service topic). This ended up a rich learning experience for all.

If early identification of a concrete and well-developed problem of practice is not possible, facilitators may suggest that the school choose something different, that is, a problem of practice for which the network is prepared. Facilitators negotiate the problem of practice to serve two needs: (1) the host school's difficulties with student learning and (2) the development of the network. Facilitators want to help a host school and need to keep an eye on network learning. For example, if host schools decide for whatever reason to repeatedly focus on the same problem of practice (math talk, say), network learning will suffer. Variation helps network development.

EXHIBIT 2.4

Examples of Problems of Practice

- In what ways and to what extent are students engaged in their learning?
- Is learning a mutual endeavor? Are students who are sitting in groups helping each other learn? Do both teachers and students learn from each other?
- What responsibility are students taking for their own learning?
- We would like to provide academic challenge for each child. What can you observe to help us accomplish this goal?

Common Difficulties in Writing a Problem of Practice

Anxious schools can often run into trouble when attempting to write a problem of practice. Sometimes, they fall into these traps without really realizing it. Let's look at two.

Occasionally, host schools focus on teachers as their subject for the problem of practice. Many of these schools try to construct a problem of practice around observing whether teachers are properly implementing a program. A facilitator may hear a principal say that the school has been working on implementing a new approach to writing, and he or she wants to know if teachers are implementing the steps of the approach as prescribed in the in-service.

Given the long history of blaming teachers for poor student learning, facilitators should anticipate that the network might occasionally be asked to focus on teachers and to evaluate their performance. It is unfortunate how pervasive this attitude is, from politicians to educators themselves: that if only teachers did a better job, education problems would be solved. Too many educators have accepted this frame of reference, which means that a part of your work is to change mentalities.

Rounds work certainly doesn't back off from a goal of effective instruction, but not through evaluation. Rounds is descriptive and analytic. And teachers are only one part, albeit the most important part, of the instructional core. Teachers are far too often unreasonably challenged by pacing guides that require them to cover much too much content, much too quickly, for district-wide recall and understanding assessment tests. An audit rarely engages school staff in a culture of inquiry based on comprehensive evidence or a shared commitment to action necessary for school and system-wide improvement. Audits may serve a purpose in supervision or evaluation, but not in rounds.

Facilitators need to turn attention toward descriptive analysis of student learning problems rather than teacher performance. Asking the host school to rethink the suggested problem of practice in terms of student learning is a start. If the school team suggests a problem of practice around differentiated instruction, ask the school to explain the learning problem that differentiated instruction solves. One school's response was that it would get students engaged.

Differentiation is not the only way to solve problems of student engagement and may not be the best. A focus on one teacher method (differentiation) eliminates other possible solutions for discussion. A focus on student learning problems increases potential solutions. As Elizabeth City describes in "Learning from

Instructional Rounds" (*Educational Leadership* 69 [October 2011]), it is possible for an effective problem of practice to focus on teacher behaviors. She lists twelve common problems of practice, three of which examine teacher behaviors. None, however, are audits of teacher performance.

In any case, it is essential that students be the subject of inquiry for the first several rounds to shift member thinking from teacher behavior to what is happening in the classroom in light of what students make, do, say, or write.

There are no other forms of observable student evidence that we can use in rounds work other than describing what students make, do, say, or write (Esther Care and Patrick Griffin, "Assessment Is for Teaching," *Independence* 34 [October 2009]). Observation of these student behaviors is crucial to culture change in which accountability is based on the development of thinking and learning of students, in much the same way that accountability in the medical profession is based upon the wellness of patients.

Sometimes, a host school suggests a problem of practice that is actually designed to ask network members to observe what the school already believes to be strong practice, hoping the network will be impressed by the great teaching and learning going on in its classrooms. Most principals and faculty who host a productive rounds visit have very mixed feelings about volunteering. Nonetheless, they must leave themselves open to objective observation during rounds visits. Facilitators need to emphasize on their initial meetings with host schools (and again to the entire network during the launch session) that rounds is a continuous improvement model, not a remedial model only for underperforming schools. Schools should volunteer out of an interest to improve faculty and student learning. They will most benefit when they regard rounds as an opportunity for self-improvement through objective observational feedback from their colleagues.

A principal of a magnet school once expressed surprise at feedback that described a school-wide pattern of students sitting in groups, but working as individuals. The overall picture suggested the school, a school of choice that emphasized student team projects, had much work to do.

At the end of the rounds session, the principal, fully in agreement with the documented findings, thanked her network colleagues for their hard work and then admitted she had anticipated nothing but praise. It was not that the principal was uninterested in improvement or misunderstood the purpose of rounds; it was that this was the first time she saw clearly what was happening in her school. Nonetheless, she hadn't really expected the rounds visit to be so forthright.

She and her school overcame this thinking by volunteering again two years later for further self-inquiry by posing a problem of practice that took advantage of all the network had to offer. This commitment to self-improvement marked a turning point in their school culture.

To be alert to this kind of problem, facilitators should determine whether the school has identified an authentic problem of practice; they can do so by asking the school for evidence about its learning problem. If a potential host school has difficulty demonstrating learning problems through test data or other objective measures, the facilitator should conclude that the school might not be ready for hosting a rounds visit. In this case, the facilitator should consider whether the school should rethink its choice of a problem of practice or whether another school would be a better volunteer.

Expect to spend more time helping the first host school craft this question, because of its lack of prior in-service on rounds. This problem of practice will be what you'll be using in your launch session as a training exercise to show network members how to focus their observations during simulated video classroom visits. This problem of practice carries additional importance because it provides the network with the basis for its first rounds visit and will be viewed as a model.

Preparing the Host School's Presentation to the Network

Before leaving the pre-rounds host school meeting, you as the facilitator should prepare the host principal to make a brief presentation to the network (which, if it is for any rounds visit other than the first, will be done at the rounds session prior to the one their school will host). A version of this same presentation, actually more like a reminder and update, will also be made on the morning of the rounds visit. These two presentations will essentially cover the same material. Assure the principal that the presentation is not a big deal—that it should be understood as a short and informal introduction that does not require much preparation.

You then review the relevant elements. The presentations should begin with the principal's introduction of the problem of practice and why it was chosen. Next, the principal should establish some context for the issue by providing a sketch of pertinent information, such as student and teacher demographics, current school improvement efforts, and whatever issues are of particular interest to the host school staff. Suggest that the principal anticipate questions around the school's problem of practice. The time frame for this presentation is never more than about five to seven minutes. You should reassure a nervous principal that the requirements of the presentation can be satisfied by offering a summary of highlights from the conference you and the internal rounds leadership team have just had, or you can volunteer to assist the principal to present if desired.

Preparing the Network

Once the rounds process is well established, you may want to begin preparing exercises for your network around the upcoming problem of practice. Ideally, at each rounds visit of the network, the principal of the upcoming school to host the next visit will present that school's problem of practice. This is to allow members to get up to speed, if necessary, to observe more purposefully in the classroom.

There is no such thing as a perfect problem of practice. Even though nearly all schools struggle continuously to improve student learning, not all schools struggle in the same way or with the same issues. And problems of practice are often in flux as new data arises and as progress or the lack thereof occurs.

LAST WORDS

The pre-rounds host school meeting serves multiple purposes: to establish a functional working link between networks and host schools; to help host schools prepare for rounds; and for facilitator diagnosis of school and network member readiness to do rounds work. During the meeting, facilitators also begin their own mental calculation about how much and what kind of work will realistically be required for rounds to result in improved learning.

If it is possible for the superintendent (or convening authority) to determine the host schools for the first few visits right at the outset, this will be helpful to planning for all concerned. Advance school selections allow you to work with each school's leadership in the weeks (or months) ahead of every rounds visit to prepare a problem of practice and to prepare the network members.

Facilitator interests in the school's problem of practice are far-reaching. A problem of practice says a lot about a school. Is this a culture in which decisions are based on the needs of the adult or the student? Do schools have data teams with knowledge of how to zero in on student learning problems to create productive problems of practice? (If not, work described in Kathryn Parker Boudett and coauthors' *Data Wise: Using Assessment Results to Improve Teaching and Learning*, Revised and Expanded Edition, published by Harvard Education Press in 2013, should be considered for the school's potential in-service in conjunction with rounds.) Other factors to consider are whether leadership teams function as non-defensive partners vitally involved with decision making. Do educators attribute student learning problems to factors that are within the school's ability to solve? What role does the faculty as a whole play in school affairs? What factors support or hinder the likelihood that rounds work will result in committed action?

Facilitators need to work hard at helping schools and networks understand that in agreeing to a rounds visit, they are committing to working together on the school's problem of practice and the network's development as instructional leaders.

CHAPTER 3

The Launch Session, Day One

The launch session is the inaugural network meeting. This is the first time network members convene as a group to learn about the skills and culture they will need as a collegial body to effect large-scale school improvement. Facilitators will want to take full advantage of this two-day training period because once the launch session is over, they are unlikely to have another block of time like this to devote solely to the concepts and skill development of rounds work.

The launch session is essentially a training session where you introduce the network members to the theory, culture, and practice of instructional rounds and the idea that improving teaching and learning at scale can only be accomplished by educational leaders dedicated to a shared practice. Their rounds work together will focus on the instructional core, defined as the interaction between teachers and students in the presence of content. You will be teaching them how to zero in on the instructional core as they look at tasks in the classroom. In teaching network members how to do this work, you will be introducing them to important skills, like how to see objectively what is happening in the classroom so that they can take observational notes of evidentiary value. You will need to provide multiple opportunities for the members to practice specific and objective observational skills because they will find it challenging to change their old ways of seeing. Traditionally, observation has been used in schools to judge and evaluate teachers through the use of checklists and standards. The various classroom analysis opportunities you offer here will reorient the members to watch for the interaction of all three elements of the instructional core—teacher, student, and content. Their past frame of reference was probably focused on the teacher, to the exclusion of all else. Because these skills are so difficult to learn on the fly in a live classroom, you will teach them through the use of video simulation exercises, a much safer space to practice learning observation skills, with the opportunity for replay and self-correction.

THE GOALS OF THE LAUNCH SESSION

The learning goals of this session include having participants begin to think of themselves as part of a fledgling network committed to learning from one another. This involves developing norms for productive network interaction. Facilitators should make the network members aware of the countercultural nature of any work that challenges the status quo of private practice. Their first job will be to shed a culture of nice to achieve a mind-set rooted in unbiased inquiry and to understand the context, purpose, and stages of rounds. They will need to approach the work willing to take responsibility for what they produce and to confront obstacles within themselves and the current culture that prevent them from being straightforward about what they see. All of this is in the service of preparing for their boots-on-the-ground first school rounds visit.

THE IMPORTANCE OF PACING

Because of time constraints and the heavy learning demands of this session, pacing is important. In introducing new content, facilitators should remember it is more important to pause frequently and give the network members time to reflect and discuss than it is to cover everything. The morning is about learning the theory, and the afternoon is about the practice, when they will learn by doing. True understanding of the power of the rounds process won't come until the network is a few months and rounds visits into the work. This is a developmental process that many find frustrating. Facilitators need to encourage while pressing them on. Tell them to be patient and trust the process. It will get easier, they will get better, and understanding will come. They just need time.

REFRAMING THE PRACTICE

As a facilitator, you begin work on developing a shared practice in the launch session by introducing links between school context, education research, and purposeful, objective observation in the classroom. Most educators are woefully unaware of what research has to say about best practices for teaching and learning. One important goal is to take a step to correcting this by having the network develop over time an informed, mutually agreed-upon understanding of the nature of effective instruction.

Rounds is conducted with an objective, yet respectful frame of reference. This begins in the launch session and is modeled by facilitators. You must remain firm about not allowing the authority or comfort level of adults to get in the way of what is needed to improve learning. Much as the best measure of medical practice is the progress of patients, facilitators focus accountability around student learning. Education would be quite different if the lack of learning success of a single student was met with the same kind of action as that which a medical rounds team takes over the decline of a single patient.

The entire focus of this work is the instructional core. The authors of *Instructional Rounds* refer to the instructional core as anchoring the work. You will find that when you introduce this thought-provoking material in the launch session, there will be skeptics among the members. This can be a great opportunity to move the work forward. Doubts and questions should always be regarded as moments that can inspire deep thinking from members and trigger a rethinking of assumptions. This is exactly what you hope to accomplish.

THE AGENDA

This chapter and the following offer a chronological look at the two-day launch session. In this chapter, I cover the steps of the first day, beginning with a quick overview of instructional rounds as a form of school improvement. I give a quick tour of this material, describing the instructional core and how to use it as an instrument for school reform. I review why a formal and shared understanding of terms such as *student engagement* is so important, show how to encourage participants to develop their own network norms, and explain why these are critical to guiding network behavior and developing a productive culture to achieve success. The afternoon's curriculum uses video exercises to concentrate on the discipline of learning to see. The first day ends with a network debrief. (See exhibit 3.1 for the launch session agenda.)

The agenda for the launch session covers two eight-hour days of training. Each section of the agenda builds upon the prior, beginning with an introduction to the theory and concepts of instructional rounds, and then moving into learning observational skills through training exercises that teach observational, analytical, and implementation skills.

EXHIBIT 3.1

Two-Day Network Launch Session Agenda
Introduction to Instructional Rounds

First Day

8:00–8:30	Registration and refreshments
8:30–9:00	Welcome, introduction, review of agenda and goals, and warm-up exercise
9:00–9:45	Introduction to instructional rounds: overview of a rounds visit; what rounds is and is not; why do rounds; why a network; how rounds fits into the scheme of schooling
9:45–10:15	Research review on leadership and factors that influence student learning
10:15–10:45	Break
10:45–11:45	Defining the instructional core and its role in school reform
11:45–12:30	Discussion of fears, hopes, and network norms that guide the behavior of network members; recruitment of think-tank members to assist with developing network norms
12:30–1:00	Lunch break
1:00–1:30	Developing the discipline of seeing, part 1: observation exercises in whole and small groups; analyzing and categorizing observation evidence
1:30–2:00	Developing the discipline of seeing, continued: observing and analyzing video paused at key points for sharing evidence aloud. "What did you see?"
2:00–2:15	Break
2:15–3:00	Developing a definition of student engagement: participants work in small groups
3:00–3:45	Developing the discipline of seeing, continued: observing and analyzing a second video; begin rounds simulation with a problem of practice
3:45–4:00	Debrief and reflection: delta/plus exercise: pluses (what helped learning), deltas (changes needed), and lingering questions

There may be reasons to limit a launch session to one day: it can serve as an adequate introduction to small groups of new staff coming on board, a bit of in-service for faculty or specialists, or as a demonstration of a rounds experience for specific groups. But to actually prepare a full-fledged network for rounds work, a limited launch time results in limited network and skill development. Participants are less prepared to conduct rounds, relationships and norms have little staying power, and facilitators have less time to inform members about the next steps for implementation. I don't recommend it.

PRELIMINARIES: AN INTRODUCTORY LETTER

The first step in planning the launch session is sending an introductory letter to the rounds network. The letter should be sent as soon as the facilitator has met with the convening authority, come to agreement on job functions and conditions, and ascertained the district goals and expectations for instituting a rounds network. The letter may come from the district or from the facilitator. It should inform the network of the place and time of the first meeting, describe goals, and frame expectations around commitment and attendance. (See "Sample Introductory Letter for Facilitators" in appendix A.)

A MORNING OF LEARNING ABOUT ROUNDS

Most workshops are based on an 8 a.m. to 4 p.m. schedule, but district contracts must be taken into account. The first half hour is set aside for registration and greetings. As participants arrive, they receive table assignments and a folder of handouts, including the agenda and to be completed during the session. Seating is arranged by the convening authority in tables of five to seven members, for the greatest possible range of grade levels and positions at each table. The tables allow viewing for a PowerPoint presentation and are big enough to accommodate a supply of materials, poster paper, and personal belongings, but are not so big or so close together that intimate discussion among tablemates is made difficult. See the materials list in exhibit 3.2.

When it is time to begin, you might ask the district superintendent or other hiring authority to convene the group and open the meeting. In this way, you are introduced as a facilitator rather than as the overall authority. Since both the facilitator and the network members will have to demand of themselves high standards

---

EXHIBIT 3.2

Materials and Technology Needed for Launch Session and Rounds Visits

- Chart or poster paper and lots of wall space for display purposes
- Masking tape or blue tack for posting work products on the walls
- Chart stands (not necessary with adequate wall space)
- Markers of assorted colors (thick and dark colors are best)
- Name tags (large), with first names in bold
- Table numbers (with stands if available) to make it easy to find seats and reassign groups
- PowerPoint projector, computer, screen or clean wall for video images; extension cord; speakers for video replays; microphone if needed
- Very large supply of three-by-three-inch yellow sticky notes
- Red-colored sticky dots about one-quarter inch wide for use on chart or poster paper
- Handouts (originals to be provided by the facilitator and sent in advance for copying)
- Confidential meeting space large enough to accommodate eight to ten tables and comfortable movement to and from the tables; each table should fit four to six participants generously and be large enough for spreading out poster paper.
- A separate table for the facilitator, with enough space to spread out presentation materials
- A pad of white lined paper and pen for each participant for notes (some may use electronic devices)

---

and strict adherence to rounds discipline, it is important to have the facilitating role seen in the light of a rounds purist rather than a boss. Avoid using a stage, and don't let a podium get between the network and you. This day initiates the relationship between the facilitator and the network, and setting the right tone is important. In this same way, the network should identify and bond as a group that takes care of each other while demanding the best of one another.

The first goal is for network members to get to know each other in the context of shared problem solving, the exchange of ideas, a coming to consensus, and the development of norms. This can be a good time for you to share your own goals as facilitator: that the network members create an open door to a new educational culture. They will need to dedicate themselves to a shared practice of teaching and learning and reject the traditionally private practice of educators. As Joseph McDonald and coauthors explain in *The Power of Protocols: An Educator's Guide to Better Practice* (2nd edition, Teachers College Press, 2007, page 106), "being transparent and open about what you are trying allows for . . . opportunities to talk about the results afterwards. And the courage you show enables participants to become engaged, and helps build community."

When you begin self-introductions, ask members to comment about the extent of their knowledge about instructional rounds and what they hope to gain from taking part in this experience. Occasionally someone will claim to have taken part in what he or she will call instructional rounds. This is fine. This person will be a great help to newer members if in fact it is instructional rounds as it is understood here. Now is the time to begin to sort out some of the differences between an instructional rounds network and other methods of classroom observation like walkthroughs.

After introductions, it's time to review the day's agenda and learning goals, which include understanding instructional rounds and the instructional core, the steps of the rounds process, and developing group norms.

Explaining Instructional Rounds

You need to help members understand the uniqueness of instructional rounds, what it is and isn't, the reasons for conducting rounds and forming a network, and how rounds fits into school improvement. It is a fairly radical departure from the way most educators approach their practice. A culture and shared practice based upon observation and analysis is unlike past attempts at educational improvement, such as walkthroughs, evaluations, and supervision. Because many network members have no current frame of reference for what they will be doing, they will need to keep an open mind. It can help to discuss the medical model upon which rounds is based so that the members can transfer the concept of medical rounds to the education profession.

Involving the Network Members

You begin by asking each table to choose a facilitator who will be tasked with encouraging all participants in discussion, keeping an eye on time requirements for exercises, and ensuring that the group stays on track. Table facilitators represent another way that network members can take responsibility for the process and their own learning. You then begin a discussion of what it means to be part of a network; why a network is necessary for improving learning at scale; how rounds, as a process and not a program, is different from other learning improvement efforts; and the reasons for doing rounds at all. Later in the morning, you will be asking the members to develop norms for their work together as a network for the coming year. At that time, the members should share personal thoughts about rounds and what it means to be a member of the network. Once this discussion gets going as an entire group, ask the members to finish it at their tables and share their thinking aloud to the whole group at the end. This is just the beginning of what will be many opportunities to gain clarity about the meaning of network membership, and it is an important first step. It's a good idea to circulate during these conversations, urging table facilitators to exercise their duties and asking how the discussion is going.

Connecting Research to Practice

The next section of the morning agenda is devoted to looking at the latest educational research findings and how such objective data and research are critical strategic partners to school improvement. (Like this discussion, nearly all network rounds visits have a short, relevant, but separate professional development segment, or in-service component on topics of best practice and varying interest.) The medical model that values well-trained, up-to-date medical care again serves as a useful metaphor for stressing the importance of educators who are equally well versed in the field's latest research findings and most effective techniques. Knowing what recent research has to say about productive teaching and learning can inform how members think about their profession when they visit the classroom.

In discussing some of the latest education research findings, you might ask members whether they would visit doctors who ignored the latest research and medical advances. Don't we owe it to our students, then, to be aware of what recent research says works best?

At this point, I often quote from Australian educator John Hattie's 2012 book, *Visible Learning for Teachers*, which is replete with insight into research-proven successful teaching strategies. Hattie discusses the value of looking at what is embedded in all strategies. Rather than "implement only the top strategies . . . it is important to understand the underlying reasons for the success of the strategies and use this as the basis for making decisions about teaching methods . . . These top strategies rely on the influence of peers, feedback, transparent learning intentions and success criteria, teaching multiple strategies or teaching using various strategies, and attending to both surface and deep knowing" (p. 84).

To introduce the importance of research, I often introduce an exercise called Influences on Achievement, which draws on Hattie's meta-analysis of over eight hundred research studies involving over 240 million students. (The exercise is described in greater detail in appendix B; see "Exercise: Influences on Achievement.") In this exercise, table facilitators distribute a list of interventions that have been shown to have an effect on student learning. The list is arranged alphabetically, and participants are asked to rate the effectiveness of each intervention (low, medium, or high). After comparing their ratings in small groups, table facilitators distribute a second document, which categorizes the same interventions in order of their effectiveness, based on Hattie's research. The exercise is intended to explore the members' knowledge of educational research and to surface and possibly challenge some of their assumptions about effective teaching. It can also be very helpful in identifying topics for future in-service sessions. For instance, the participants may be surprised to learn that giving feedback is more important than asking questions. That provides an opportunity to ask for volunteers to research effective feedback as background reading for an in-service discussion at the next rounds meeting.

Rounds is an inquiry process about the cause and effect of interactions within the instructional core. Members aware of education research will be able to think more broadly and more objectively about what they see in the classroom. Network members find this particular exercise fun, interesting, and motivating and often ask for extra copies to use in faculty meetings.

After the exercise, the facilitator opens the floor to a whole-group discussion by asking if there were any surprises or questions about the research. You need not have all the answers, but you should take the opportunity to point to resources for further study. (I often bring Hattie's books as well as others of interest for reference to this session.) The purpose here is to generate interest in research and give participants a sense of their personal level of research knowledge as a way to spur further study and make them aware of what they need to learn.

Remember, in the short time you have over these two days to bring your network up to speed, don't overwhelm people—less is truly more. Facilitators should prioritize exercises in case time runs short. Some exercises work well as standalone activities and so can be held for another time. New facilitators may find it helpful to try exercises with test groups before the launch session.

DEFINING THE INSTRUCTIONAL CORE

After a midmorning break to allow members a moment to decompress, it is time to move on to the most important and central focus of institutional rounds work: the instructional core (exhibit 3.3).

The heart of the thesis of instructional rounds is that there is no way to understand what is happening in the classroom without looking at the interactions between the student and teacher in the presence of content. One part of this triad cannot be understood without seeing how it relates to the other two. If you change one element of the core, you have to change all three. You must emphasize that the only entry points to improving learning at scale are directly through the core and that all rounds work involves the core—from classroom observations through to the theory of action that describes the next level of work in school improvement. *Instructional Rounds* explains the idea of the instructional core in terms of the following key principles described in exhibit 3.4.

In presenting each of these key principles, you will need to give members time to digest and discuss. This portion of the morning's agenda should not be rushed, because the core is central to the concepts of rounds and teaching and learning.

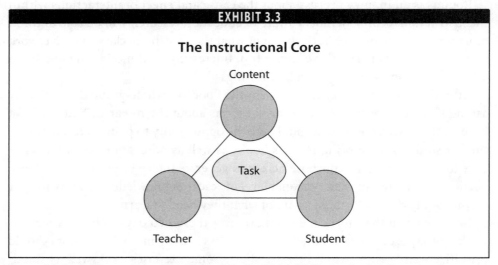

EXHIBIT 3.3

The Instructional Core

Source: Adapted with permission from Elizabeth A. City, Richard F. Elmore, Sarah E. Fiarman and Lee Teitel, *Instructional Rounds in Education: A Network Approach to Improving Teaching and Learning* (Cambridge, MA: Harvard Education Press, 2009).

EXHIBIT 3.4

The Seven Principles of the Instructional Core

1. Increases in student learning occur only as a consequence of improvements in the level of content, teachers' knowledge and skill, and student engagement.

2. If you change any single element of the instructional core, you have to change the other two.

3. If you can't see it in the core, it's not there.

4. Task predicts performance.

5. The real accountability system is in the tasks that students are asked to do.

6. We learn to do the work by doing the work, *not* by telling other people to do the work, *not* by having done the work at some point in the past, and *not* by hiring experts who act as proxies for our knowledge about how to do the work.

7. Description before analysis, analysis before prediction, prediction before evaluation.

You should anticipate that for members new to the material, a full understanding of the complexity of the core won't come until after they have experienced many rounds visits and reflected on their own personal practice.

You will overhear a number of things in member table discussions that reveal the struggle they are having in processing many of these ideas. This is healthy. For example, members often are confused by the second principle ("If you change one element of the instructional core, you have to change the other two") because their perspective on increasing learning is likely to be premised solely on teacher action to the exclusion of the need to change the cognitive demand of the content or the role of the student in learning. Student learning cannot improve unless students take more responsibility for their learning—teachers do most of the work in typical American classrooms. Another stumbling point is the third principle ("If you can't see it in the core, it isn't there"). Learning is visible in many ways, as those experienced with rounds have found by looking at what students are actually doing in relation to what they are being asked to do. Without command of rounds observation techniques, however, people new to rounds have difficulty understanding how it is possible to "see" learning.

The Students' Role

Regarding how to conceptualize the student role, members often rely on a proposition called *gradual release of responsibility*, which relies on having teachers yield responsibility bit by bit to students as a way to have them take more responsibility for their own learning. Facilitators should challenge this thinking. The gradual-release dynamic is far more effective viewed in reverse as a gradual increase of responsibility. When restated, this view focuses on the students' acquiring of greater responsibility for their learning. It is not that teachers release responsibility for what takes place in the classroom—this is not appropriate. Instead, learning is improved when a teacher creates the circumstances for students to assume greater responsibility for their own learning.

The teacher's job is to take responsibility for restructuring content, changing the accountability system in the classroom, and redirecting teacher and student roles in such a way that students do the work. Responsibility in the classroom is not a zero-sum game. The sphere of teacher responsibility does not decrease as student responsibility increases. Both spheres of responsibility increase simultaneously. Teachers must always take responsibility for what takes place in the classroom.

Distinguishing Between Content, Assignment, and Task

Facilitators should help the network members understand the difference between assignment and task to sharpen observation skills about the level of cognitive demand in the classroom around the roles of teacher and student. The assignment is what the teacher designs to accomplish the learning objective for the lesson and is represented by what the teacher asks the students to do. The task is the work the students actually do. These two are not the same thing. The way in which grade-level standards or curriculum content is translated into assignments by the teacher and unfolds in classroom lessons during instruction, followed by the work the students actually do, creates the opportunity (or not) for student thinking to develop. As portrayed in exhibit 3.5, this evolution of the cognitive demand of content (represented by the first rectangle) is translated by the teacher into assignments (the second rectangle) and finally is translated by the teacher and student interaction into the work the students actually do (the third rectangle), a process that often results in a deterioration of cognitive demand. Students' opportunity to learn consequently diminishes as each step in the translations unfolds.

This diagram is particularly helpful in preparing participants for the video observations later in the afternoon. Facilitators will want to emphasize the importance

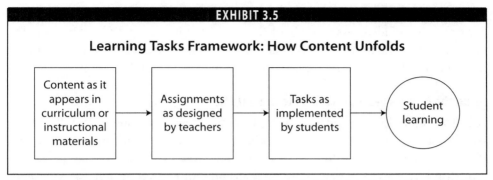

EXHIBIT 3.5

Learning Tasks Framework: How Content Unfolds

of the distinction between assignment and task, and encourage observers to consider the level of cognitive demand of each.

Facilitators can help members develop better observation skills by alerting them to observe for subtle differences between what students actually do and the stated learning intention or assignment given. Research shows that with originally high-cognitive-demand material, only about one-third remains at this high level as students engage with the material (Mary Kay Stein et al., "Implementing Standards-Based Mathematics Instruction," in *Secondary Lenses on Learning: Team Leadership for Mathematics in Middle and High Schools*, ed. Catherine Miles Grant et al. [Thousand Oaks, CA: Corwin, 2009], 245). It is the work students actually do, not what teachers do per se, that predicts performance and determines what and how well students learn.

DEVELOPING NORMS

Setting clear expectations and norms is essential for the success of rounds work. Network cultural norms guide the work from beginning to end. For this reason, and to develop network ownership of rounds work, the network members must create their own norms.

The group's norms will guide the development of collegial, shared responsibility for the work only to the extent that the members are willing to invest in them. It will take three or four rounds at a minimum and more than a year for some networks to develop the level of trust and feeling of safety that allows for a real confrontation of ideas. As time goes by, it is easy to forget how difficult it was in the beginning. As one first-year principal noted, it was only after three rounds meetings that he felt he could fully participate in the debate and discussion.

Using the Group's Fears and Hopes to Draw Up Norms

All ideas should be considered, and all dissident voices respected. A facilitator should model this throughout the work. While network members discuss values they hold important for the network, they must try to develop explicitly worded guidelines. Norms are intended to be revisited and revised in light of experience as the work progresses.

Ask the table groups to brainstorm and compile answers for the following two questions to sort out their expectations and concerns for building trust, safety, honest communication, and productive action. Be sure to explain that norms are created to help ensure that their hopes for school improvement are realized and that their fears don't come true.

- What are your fears about engaging in a network and doing this work?
- What do you hope will take place if this were to be the best and most productive work you and the network could do? (See *The Power of Protocols*, pages 23–27; and *Instructional Rounds*, pages 146–150.)

Once the group's fears and hopes are presented, members begin the following protocol for developing written norms, which the facilitator starts by asking: "Given our fears and hopes, what will we need to do to allay our fears and increase the likelihood that this will be the best professional development possible?"

The work on norms is not placed earlier on the agenda, because the members can't begin writing them without (1) understanding what rounds is all about and (2) having had the opportunity to get to know each other over the exchange of ideas. The norms represent what the members will be asking of each other so that all the participants can gain from the work. The norms support shared practice with shared responsibility—the learning culture of the network.

Norms As Guidelines for Working Relationships

The development of norms cannot anticipate all possible circumstances, and they are not about imposing a set of rules. They are guidelines for working relationships. Inform the members that a norm is no more than one sentence and should be explicitly clear in its meaning and intention. Norms are stated as positives, describing what the group agrees should happen versus what should not happen. For example, you might write "Encourage everyone to take a turn," instead of "Don't monopolize group time." Exhibit 3.6 lists nine potential topics you can display for network consideration without any requirement that such topics be addressed. The list is only intended to promote comprehensive discussion.

Using Gallery Walks to Generate the Group's Norms

The table groups should generate perhaps three to ten items on poster paper to put on the wall for others to read. We call postings around the room for strolling readers *gallery walks*. This technique also allows for some much-needed physical movement as well as reflection. Putting up the work as soon as a group finishes also subtly encourages slower groups to accelerate their contributions. You can also encourage more timely completion by quietly asking a group how much time they need to finish when other groups are waiting. When all the members are done, facilitators ask each group to present its thoughts to the gathered network, meanwhile asking what items the members see in common, what items seem to be especially important, and so on. This can be accomplished while all are standing in front of the gallery or after the members return to their seats.

EXHIBIT 3.6

Things to Consider When Drawing Up Network Norms

- The importance of how the network functions
- The nature of confidentiality
- Varying levels of expertise and knowledge
- Personal feelings of safety in doing the work
- Conduct or behavior in sessions
- A culture of nice versus productive learning
- Commitment levels to rounds, long and short term
- The use of communication devices
- Other

Creating a Think Tank for Finalizing the Norms

Creating network norms is critical work and will take longer to develop than is possible during the time devoted to this agenda item. To overcome the time issue and to ensure network ownership of the final product, facilitators should seek a small group of four to seven member volunteers to form an ad hoc think tank. This think tank must be willing to convene at lunch, the end of the day, or before the beginning of the session on the next day to distill and refine the suggestions for norms created by the table groups. At the end of the second day, you will be asking if there are volunteers interested to serve on the more permanent think tank, as described in chapter 1. So the creation of the ad hoc think tank now serves to provide members with an initial model of some of the work a think tank does.

The think-tank volunteers on this day are charged with presenting a final list of no more than five to ten items for the network's consideration as the first thing the next morning. They will explain their thinking and invite questions and comments. This is when a facilitator could remind the think-tank members that a camel is a horse invented by committee, and their charge is to present the network with a horse. Their write-ups don't necessarily have to be adopted the next morning, but whether or not further work is required, the network will want the norms to be agreed upon and printed out before the first school rounds visit.

What Happens When Norms Aren't Followed

Norms may seem unimportant until the need for them arises. A forty-person Australian network I was facilitating was finalizing the wording on confidentiality, their last norm, when one of the network principals called out, "Just checking, but I assume confidentiality doesn't apply to positive comments? Like the good ideas in another school's classroom, which I'd like to share with the teachers in my own school?"

There were groans as another colleague spoke up. "Mate," he said, "let me put it this way: What happens in Vegas stays in Vegas."

A month later, as I was checking in with the host principal about a network visit the previous day, she, visibly angry, said that one of her star teachers had discovered that the work in her classroom was being praised in another school by a rounds network principal. After listening a moment, I asked if she was comfortable bringing the problem to the network.

After hearing the story, network members were apologetic, but curious why a respected teacher would be upset about praise. In discussing it, they brought forth a number of possible reasons:

- We had promised that observations were for our own professional development.
- The teacher may not want to be "the tall poppy" (pointed out as better than her colleagues).
- If we gossip about the good lessons, the participants might fear that we'd also blab about the bad.
- This whole observation thing wasn't supposed to be about judging what's good or what's bad.
- We had agreed that our observations would be kept confidential among ourselves.

Having the host principal open the discussion by sharing this story was quite helpful, and the network grew stronger because of it. It's an important issue. Honesty and trust are foundational principles. Members, host schools, everyone, need to be able to trust their colleagues to honor confidentiality if they are to feel safe about sharing openly. The work of the entire network could be jeopardized if members were perceived as untrustworthy. In any case, these debates are not something for you as facilitator to solve. Your job is to stand back and assist communication as the network struggles with it. Your only comment might be to ask whether they want to frame it in terms of some kind of norm they can all own and perhaps have the think tank draft something for consideration.

AFTERNOON OF PRACTICE

The afternoon's agenda is primarily about teaching network members the hands-on skills necessary to becoming skilled classroom observers.

The Discipline of Seeing, and an Observation Exercise

In this part of the session, the participants will take part in an exercise to practice observing, taking notes on what they see and classifying portions of notes transcribed by others through watching a video of a classroom in action. The aim here is to teach the network how to describe objectively what they see, without judgment and with fine-grained specificity. The facilitator will need to make sure the network members are alert to ambiguous words, jargon, or meaningless descriptions such as "teacher centered."

To begin this work, you can use an exercise called "From Observation to Evidence" to help members define what it means to see objectively. The exercise is adapted from *Instructional Rounds*.

In this exercise, the facilitator distributes a list of classroom observations that participants are asked to classify as either specific/fine-grained, and objective/non-judgmental, or not. Items must be both specific and objective to be considered evidence. Ask each table group to come to consensus on the classification of the items as either viable evidence or not. Once the teams have agreed on which items qualify as evidence and which do not, share with the entire group how you have categorized them, with the qualification that there are degrees of how specific or objective an item may be. Discuss how each item is properly classified, not for scoring purposes but to develop the parameters of what makes useful evidence and what does not. Help the members learn by asking them what would improve a too-general or too-judgmental piece of evidence. This exercise also prepares the participants for classroom observation by teaching them to capture usable observation notes as evidence for analysis of what is transpiring in the classroom. (For a sample list of observations, see "Exercise: From Observation to Evidence," in appendix C.)

USING VIDEOS FOR OBSERVATION TRAINING

Once the exercise is completed, the facilitator moves on to show videos that simulate authentic classroom experiences for the network to practice taking specific and objective notes. One advantage of video observation is that everyone has a front-row seat, so to speak, which provides a controlled opportunity for disciplined skill development—an opportunity that is lost once live observations begin. (As soon as the observation teams enter classrooms and spread out around the room, everyone sees and hears different things.)

Videos of classroom scenes are terrific for developing observation and note-taking skills because all the members see the same action and can discuss what they see unhindered by the need for confidentiality or carefully chosen words that could offend. The caveat to bring to the network's attention is that videos do not render a full picture of classroom interactions and students cannot be questioned, thereby limiting understanding of what is occurring. But it is precisely this controlled simplicity that makes the videos appropriate teaching tools. There are many videos online and on the market. See "Sources for Classroom Teaching Videos" in appendix D for more information.

Video training works well to teach this work, which is why it's a good idea to present a minimum of three videos that cover a variety of teaching and learning scenarios for observation training. The video selections should be based on two criteria: their note-taking challenges and the extent to which they model productive teaching practices. These videos provide a unique group learning opportunity by offering multiple teaching and learning circumstances that bring the training closer to the diversity of the actual classroom scenes the group will be studying.

The main thrust of this session is to teach members the discipline of being careful to make observations that are specific and objective and that focus on the full range of interactions involving all three elements of the instructional core. Encourage the members to concentrate on what they see and hear in regard to all three elements: teacher, student, and content.

The First Video: Simple Observations and Specific Notes

The first video is used to introduce how to capture consequential classroom action through note taking. See exhibit 3.7 for the criteria to consider in selecting the first video.

The first work with a video clip is intended for developing descriptive language skills, with an emphasis on capturing specific and objective observation data. You should not provide a problem of practice for the first video. If the participants ask whether the note taking would have been easier if they had been given a problem of practice, you can reply that you are delighted that they understand the necessity for using a problem of practice, but that for this first exercise, they should initially focus more on capturing as much evidence as they can about the interactions of the instructional core.

The Basic Observation Skills Exercise

As you show the first video, try stopping it every 60 or 120 seconds to ask the group: "What did you see or hear?" The focus is on what they have jotted down, not what they verbally choose to report. Remind them that their notes are all they will have at the end of their school visit. When visiting four classrooms of live action in quick succession, they will be unable to accurately remember all that took place. This practice session is designed to help them learn to collect evidence through note taking that they can depend on when they are trying to analyze patterns of teaching and learning across several classrooms. Start by having someone read from his or her notes, and then ask others to check their notes for additional information until most of what happened has been identified.

Regardless of whether or not the information in this first activity seems important to the instructional core, the facilitator's focus is more on accuracy. You should

---

EXHIBIT 3.7

Requirements for the First Classroom Simulation Video

The first video introduces how to capture consequential classroom action through note taking. For this reason, look for a video that demands less complex note taking. The raw footage of typical eighth-grade math and science lessons from the United States and Australia is a good choice. These online videos are available from the free Trends in International Mathematics and Science Study (TIMSS) video collection.

What makes many of these videos appropriate is that they depict typical, not model, teaching and learning situations that show teacher-student dialogue in which the teacher asks questions that have right or wrong answers. This lack of complexity helps when the participants are first learning to take notes, so for your first video you want fairly straightforward material for network note taking. (You have not yet introduced taking notes around a problem of practice.)

Why I Choose Math Content for This Video

The TIMSS video I often screen is US87, a lesson on the interior angles of a polygon. The members groan when they learn they are being asked to gather observation data about an eighth-grade geometry lesson, because many fear they've forgotten what they may have once known about geometry. This is precisely why I've chosen this particular subject video. The point is that rounds work does not require the observer to be an expert in all subjects. When I hear someone say, "Maybe I am not qualified to observe this class. I don't think I'll be able to take notes of any value," I tell the person that all he or she needs to be of value to the team are expert observation skills, not math (or other content) ability.

---

ask if all the participants recorded the same observation, and that the members explain, define, or defend their observations, by asking: "What's the evidence?" You need to demonstrate the pursuit of high standards of specific and objective evidence that is expected of note takers. You also need to model how colleagues should question each other to achieve these high standards.

Keep an eye out for members watching the videos without writing. I am always surprised by this, but have learned that the best way to handle it is to remind the group that everyone should now be taking notes even if they are unsure exactly what to record. Part of the reason for stopping the video so often in the beginning is to help the nonrecorders hear what others have noted, minute by minute. People appreciate hearing what their colleagues note as valuable and what they consider objective and specific, as soon as we begin the lesson; it accelerates the understanding of those who may be less confident.

After stopping the video for the observation reporting at very short intervals a few times, allow the video to run for two or three minutes. As you move on with evidence sharing, ask the members in each small group to share their notes at their tables and to help each other stay in the descriptive by quizzing each other about the evidence. Then have them repeat this step for another round of sharing and discussion. If time allows, it helps to replay the video from the beginning for about ten minutes. This time, the members add to or revise their notes as needed, analyze the changes they have made, and share aloud the differences between their first set of notes and their second. This review helps the members identify their goals for improvement, which they discuss.

The participants need reassurance that it is not possible to record everything happening in a classroom and not to worry about missing something during their visit. You might want to remind them that when they visit classrooms, they will be in observation teams of three or four, and what one misses another may capture.

Focusing on Using Exact Language

Members can improve their note taking by asking themselves questions such as these: Is this specific, and why? Is this objective, and why? Am I being clear or using jargon to make these descriptions? What are the offending words? Would everyone agree on the exact meaning of the terms I'm using or the action I'm referring to? Facilitators should not hesitate to press the members to force their colleagues to use more specific observations in place of such terms as *transitions*, *interactive*, and *teacher-centered* by asking their colleagues: "What's the evidence?" These questions ask for responses that break down general words into discrete behaviors and usable evidence.

Observations have degrees of objectivity and specificity, which can make it helpful for the participants to ask each other what would make this item more objective or specific. Asking for more detail or quantifying an item can help, and generally, hands-on experience is required. This is why you need to show several videos to give the members multiple opportunities to screen evidence with their colleagues before the session ends.

Exercises for Challenging One's Bias and Assumptions

A variety of activities described in *Instructional Rounds*, pages 86–98, can help the members sort out how to make observations that are specific and objective. See also exhibit 3.8.

Some of the techniques in exhibit 3.8 work well for some members, and others less so, but I encourage facilitators to become familiar with each method. My work is a blend of some of these techniques, combined with the additional strategies I have been sharing here. For example, the "evidence ball game" is not something I use, but others use it with good results.

After conducting some of these exercises, facilitators might want to have the groups take a short break or change the activity; the work is tiring.

The Second Video: Framing Observation Through a Problem of Practice

The next video begins a rounds simulation (a third video, to be shown on the next day, will also simulate a rounds visit). An authentic simulation requires observation based on a problem of practice to focus note taking. This increases the complexity of the launch session work and develops further skills of observation. Again, the most valuable observation notes shed light on the cause-and-effect interactions of the instructional core, but this time, the observations are further focused around a problem of practice. Introducing a problem of practice demands more sophisticated seeing, but it also simplifies the process by asking the members to narrow

---

EXHIBIT 3.8

Exercises to Uncover Biases and Assumptions

The Ladder of Inference

Elizabeth A. City, Richard F. Elmore, Sarah E. Fiarman and Lee Teitel, *Instructional Rounds in Education: A Network Approach to Improving Teaching and Learning* (Cambridge, MA: Harvard Education Press, 2009), page 87, explain this exercise: "The ladder of inference can be helpful in providing both an image and a language for discussing what it means to stay in the descriptive . . . The bottom rung of the ladder is descriptive. As you move up the ladder, you get farther from the [objective] evidence and closer to your beliefs, assumptions, and conclusions.

If you start at the top of the ladder, it's hard to go back down—the other rungs are missing. If you start at the bottom of the ladder and work your way up—and you do need to go up eventually to get to recommendations for improvement—then it is easier to go back up and down, to check assumptions and beliefs, and to be clear about what the recommendations are intended to address."

What's the Evidence?

City and her coauthors in *Instructional Rounds* also suggest asking where the evidence is. This is a strategic question facilitators use and urge network members to pose to their colleagues during all stages of rounds work to build a strong evidentiary foundation.

"What's the Evidence" Ball Game

Another suggestion from *Instructional Rounds* is an exercise that can be used to coach larger groups by tossing a foam ball from one person to another. Each person in possession of the ball shares at least one piece of evidence recorded from perhaps ten minutes of video. Group members ask: "What's the evidence?" for items that seem to be climbing the ladder of inference.

Evidence Police

In this *Instructional Rounds* exercise, responsibility is randomly assigned to different members who serve as "evidence police." Their job is to enforce an evidence-only rule in their group, again by asking, "What's the evidence?" It is easier for the enforcer to help members climb back down the ladder of inference through playing a role not in their typical positions of, say, someone's superintendent, principal, or teacher. This helps separate people from practice, a distinction rounds continually tries to reinforce.

Signaling

Another *Instructional Rounds* suggestion is called signaling. Members may feel safer signaling when they hear or see judgmental (or overly general) evidence by humming or holding up a colored card. This can generate a bit of humor, which can make it a good option for more timid groups or those strongly entrenched in the land of nice.

their focus. So in starting the second video, the facilitator will tell the members to try to make their observation notes relevant to the school's problem of practice.

If the network's first school to be visited has adopted a problem of practice before the start of the launch session, this problem should be used for the simulation (as explained in chapter 2). If the host school has been unable to finalize a problem of practice, you can use a fictitious problem for the purposes of the launch session. Whether it comes from the host school or is selected by the facilitators, a problem of practice helps the members concentrate their observations around one question of student learning. As mentioned, you are ratcheting up the complexity by adding this additional challenge. The members are better able to meet this challenge by doing this task in the company of colleagues, all of whom are observing the same classroom video action. See exhibit 3.9 for examples of the videos I often like to use.

Selecting a Fictitious Problem of Practice for Simulation

If the host school's problem of practice is not yet ready, use a fictitious problem of practice from a fictitious school. Give the fictitious school a name to make it readily identifiable in discussion during the simulation, for example, the Friendly School. Generally, for the fictitious problem of practice, the facilitator will find it productive to pose the following question: "In what ways and to what extent are students engaged in their learning?"

Using a focus on this question of student engagement also inevitably involves raising the related importance of cognitive demand. Essentially, it is impossible to achieve high levels of student engagement with low levels of cognitive demand, because any educational definition has to consider engagement in terms of engaging the mind and thinking of students.

The topic of student engagement is important in the launch session for two main reasons. First, student engagement is central to rounds work. A change in the role of the students, more specifically students' engagement in their own learning, is necessary to improve learning, according to the first principle of the instructional core. Second, we know from experience that student engagement as a critical concept is defined informally in almost as many ways as there are network members.

Developing a Definition of Student Engagement

As with all problems of practice, facilitators must consider whether a network is prepared to observe. In the case of the ill-defined question of student engagement, facilitators might want to open small-group discussions by asking members to

---

EXHIBIT 3.9

Requirements for the Second and Third Classroom Simulation Videos

The second video viewed on the first day of the launch session, and the third video, shown on the second day, will be used together to simulate a rounds experience. These two classroom video visits need to be regarded as representing two classrooms in one school. Their content therefore needs to make for a coherent school practice, since the members will be pooling observation notes from these two videos for analysis on the second launch day.

These videos should offer greater note-taking challenges, such as the complexity of teacher-student, student-student, whole-class, and group interactions. I usually choose these two videos from the Lenses on Learning Facilitator's Kit videos (if the district has purchased them). Otherwise, you can select from the free Annenberg Media Collection. (See "Sources for Classroom Teaching Videos" in appendix D.)

The second video I often use (provided the network has purchased it) is *The Basic Student Budget* (video clip 5.1) from Secondary Lenses on Learning, 2009. It includes nonverbal interactions related to student learning. Because nonverbal action is important, you might pause the video around these moments to ask what the members see and hear, and then allow for communal sharing of insights and note-taking techniques to help the entire group.

A good choice for the third video, *The Border Problem*, part 1, also comes from the Secondary Lenses on Learning kit. It is similar in teaching and learning styles to those in the *Basic Student Budget* video viewed the day before. (There are several videos in this kit, all of which work well when paired.)

---

come to agreement on their own table definition of student engagement to share aloud for general discussion before proceeding with further work on this problem of practice. (You may wish to provide background material on student engagement, for example, for the network's reading prior to the start of the session.)

There are many ways to deal with this issue, but the important idea is for members to have some clarity about what and why they are observing and the kinds of evidence that could be helpful to gather for this particular problem of practice. A portion of the launch agenda should be reserved for this time to help members explore their own thinking on the topic of the problem of practice (whatever it may be) before they observe the video.

The second video of classroom action is presented as if it is the network's first classroom visit. The members will use these observation notes in conjunction with notes from the third video to be viewed on the second launch day, each screening for no more than ten to fifteen minutes. The second and third videos will constitute the entirety of observation material for the simulated rounds visit to the fictitious school, and evidence from both will be combined on the second day for analysis. It is best to stop the last video only occasionally, if at all, because you are elevating the challenge and preparing the members for the upcoming host school visit. There are no replays in real schools.

DEBRIEFING AT THE DAY'S END: USING THE PLUS/DELTA PROTOCOL FOR FEEDBACK

At the end of the day, the facilitator can ask network members for feedback, using the plus/delta protocol (see "Delta/Plus Feedback Protocol" in appendix E). Through this instrument, the facilitator can learn what they found helpful and what they think could improve their learning experience. In return, the facilitator processes their comments to share with them (for better or worse) the next day.

Facilitators should give consideration to the feedback and adjust whatever needs changing to improve the network experience. When reviewing the comments, you might find it helpful to group like-minded responses, draw up summaries, and present the results to the members the first thing the next morning. In doing this, you are of course looking to continuously improve, strengthen the shared practice of rounds work, and again model responsive teaching.

CHAPTER 4

The Launch Session, Day Two

Day two completes the launch curriculum. There is still much to learn about the ideas and mechanics of instructional rounds, and the network members will still need more time to practice what they are learning. Today, the facilitator should talk to the network members about how schools write a problem of practice and how this stated problem dictates the focus of observations in host school classrooms. They will learn how to look for patterns in the data they gather, how to make predictions from these patterns, and how to use both the data and the predictions for making targeted recommendations for addressing the school's problem of practice. Eventually, each member will craft an individual statement—a theory of action—about how the member will take a leadership role in implementing his or her own part of the improvement efforts. These important documents can be tricky to write. This is something the members will learn about today but will not yet do until they acquire more rounds experience.

It's a big day, and there is never enough time. You too will have to be on your game, for the members will need your guidance at every step. You will have to know how to pare down the material to give them exactly what they need to know, when they need to know it. They will need time to digest and process this material through discussion and targeted practice exercises.

THE AGENDA

Just as the preceding chapter outlined the first launch day, this chapter will flesh out the second day's agenda in chronological order. See exhibit 4.1.

Begin the morning's session by reviewing feedback from the previous day. The think tank members follow with a presentation of the group's norms. Then the

EXHIBIT 4.1

Two-Day Network Launch Session Agenda
Introduction to Instructional Rounds

Second Day

8:00–8:30	Refreshments
8:30–9:15	Review agenda and plus/delta feedback; think tank presents its work on norms; present protocols for visiting classrooms
9:15–10:00	Learn about a problem of practice (POP), and work with the assigned POP from the previous day (on student engagement or host school POP)
10:00–10:30	Observation of video three (the second video in the simulation exercise)
10:30–10:45	Break
10:45–12:30	Simulated rounds: participants engage in multiple activities, including analyzing evidence to form patterns from observation notes
12:30–1:00	Lunch break
1:00–2:30	Continue simulated rounds visit: review the simulation and discuss lingering questions; learn about making predictions and the next level of work; given the POP, observations, patterns, and predictions, what recommendations would you have for the school?
2:30–2:45	Break
2:45–3:00	Groups present next level of work to entire gathering
3:00–3:45	Theory of action: what is it, and what role does it play?
3:45–4:00	Debrief: prepare for school visit, and hear from school to be visited; discuss next dates; give homework assignment (practice the discipline of seeing by visiting two classrooms with a network colleague or view more videos online; TIMSS videos are available for practice work); complete session feedback in handouts

participants will learn how to develop a problem of practice by teasing a line of inquiry out of student performance data. End the morning with another session practicing observation skills using the same problem of practice employed with the second video the day before. In the afternoon, the facilitator will guide the members through a simulated postclassroom observation debriefing; show them how to analyze evidence gathered during their classroom visits; and explain how to look for patterns, make predictions, complete the next level of work, and discuss theories of action. The day will end with a few comments about their upcoming rounds visit and a short presentation by the host school's principal.

Facilitators should pay attention to pacing (and paring down) the agenda as needed. The members often find certain areas of the curriculum particularly challenging—like giving up their habitual view of school careers as jobs privileged with privacy or giving up their tendency to politely ignore examples of their colleagues' less-than-effective practices. In terms of learning rounds skills, many members struggle with making objective observations, with concentrating on what students make, do, say or write, and with using language with precise meanings. Developing all these new skills takes time.

Members have different learning styles. Those who learn better by hearing about the big picture first will generally want to understand the theory before learning about how to put it into practice. Other members comprehend theory better in reverse—by first getting a feel for the applied practice, the logistics, and nuts and bolts of instructional rounds.

Facilitators should try to design this two-day launch session with both learners in mind, while remaining flexible to the particular needs of each group. New facilitators will find their own way to hammer out a launch session that works best for them and their networks.

NORMS AND PLUS/DELTA FEEDBACK

As promised at the end of the previous day, the facilitator should share the results of the plus/delta feedback (exhibit 4.2). Reviewing the feedback from the previous day sets a nice tone to the second day. By opening the day with the members' own words—their opinions on what worked, what needs changing, and what outstanding questions remain—a facilitator gives the network claim to the emotional and intellectual space in the room. It encourages the members to share their thoughts

EXHIBIT 4.2

Sample Feedback from the Plus/Delta Exercise

Pluses

- Clarity of student engagement work
- Helpfulness of video observation exercises
- Discussion of roles and norms
- Food, environments, handouts
- Opportunities to discuss and debate and process each step with colleagues
- The importance of the instructional core

Changes

- Need more videos and more time to practice note taking
- Need more breaks; the work is hard
- Need more exercises within groups

Questions

- How to capture nonverbal stuff?
- How do schools craft problems of practice?
- How will the results of our work be implemented?
- What is the timeline for this?
- How do we get teachers on board?
- When do we get teachers involved?
- What about aides?
- How do teacher evaluations fit in with rounds?
- How do we find time for this work?

as part of a broader conversation of importance and authorizes them to take charge of their learning.

It is a good idea to look for opportunities to use something from the group's suggestions to make adjustments to your practice. For example, try to honor requests for more observation or discussion time despite an agenda that is quite tight. Or sometimes, the members want more illustration of a concept through examples. Similarly, facilitators should always be alert and responsive to cues from the participants.

The next part of the agenda belongs to the think tank, which should present the list of norms the group has distilled from yesterday's network input. The goal is to adopt the norms, but if the participants believe more work is needed, the think tank and network should decide how they might get it done in time for the rounds visit. I am often asked to review the draft to see if it is "what I want." You will want to respond to such questions by saying that the norms belong to the network, and only the network can answer such questions. The network members are responsible for what takes place in their working relationships, and it is up to them to determine whether the norms reflect their thinking and will serve as a guide for their working relationships. Now is the time for the participants to speak up.

THE PROBLEM OF PRACTICE

A problem of practice advances a question a school would like addressed to help it improve a problem of student learning. This question provides the focus for all the network classroom observations and eventual learning improvement.

All members of the network need to thoroughly understand problems of practice. Many of the members, like school principals, will eventually be involved in writing a problem of practice for their school that will actually be used by the network on a rounds visit. The network members in their entirety might eventually write one for their district.

Writing a problem of practice is a skill that takes time to develop. It is better to hold off on this lesson until the members have had time to understand the instructional core, use descriptive language, and take observational notes with a student-focused problem of practice. But they are now ready to learn about it in greater depth, so begin by discussing its essential elements. The concept of using an inquiry to focus observation on a problem of student learning is a major change of perspective for educators who have previously focused on problems of teacher performance. By learning about the instructional core and the value of collecting objective observations, network members have learned some of the essentials that make up a rich problem of practice. The essentials are that it must focus on the core and be observable, actionable, and applicable across a school or district.

Although the school that is serving as host for the first network visit may have generated a problem of practice in preparation for the visit, this skill will be a new one for all the other members of the network. It's helpful to review the definition of a problem of practice and its purpose. The facilitator should then discuss the characteristics of a true problem of practice. (See chapter 2 for the definition of a problem of practice and the description of its key elements.)

Unusable Problems of Practice

Participants sometimes understand better what goes into a strong problem of practice by looking first at poorly developed problems of practice. You might offer them the following examples of problems of practice:

- Are teachers implementing the writing process?
- We would like to improve student performance in language arts. What are students doing and saying? What are teachers doing and saying?
- How well are low-income students responding to differentiated instruction?
- To what extent are students engaged in higher-order thinking?

In terms of what is wrong with the three top queries, the participants should recognize that the first question is an audit of whether teachers are doing what they are told to do, the second is too general to be of much use, and the third can't be observed. The final sample is derived from student progress data and functions as a true inquiry, making it a useful problem of practice.

It's worth spending time to discuss what it would take to improve the flawed examples. This is always instructive. The three ineffective problems of practice are questions that nearly all new members might write as a first effort. By attempting to fix these samples, the members will learn what critical pieces of information are needed to turn these questions into observable and actionable lines of inquiry.

An Exercise for Rating Problems of Practice

It is often helpful to follow this discussion with another useful exercise that asks the small groups to come to consensus on organizing a list of samples from the least to the most productive, on a scale of 1 (low) to 6 (high). See exhibit 4.3 for examples

EXHIBIT 4.3

Analyzing the Productivity Level of Sample Problems of Practice

As described in the text, the facilitator can ask the network participants to sort the following problems of practice according to the members' assessment of suitability for improving student learning.

A. Our students' performance is lower than we think it should be. We believe that if the students completed their homework, they would do better in school. During the past two months, the faculty members have taken steps on their own to improve completion of homework. What evidence is there that the students are responding?

B. We set a goal to improve student writing according to test results and classroom performance. What are the teachers doing and saying in writing instruction? What are the students doing and saying?

C. We have conducted a faculty in-service on implementing a new math curriculum. However, we have seen no change in student understanding of mathematics. The students do not seem to be making connections between the lessons and math tasks, problem solving in particular. The teachers do not understand why. What evidence do you see of student understanding and ability to do the math assigned?

D. Our students expressed a disconnection to the school in the student survey, and our students seem less interested or motivated to learn than we would hope. We have been working on presenting lessons in a variety of hands-on, active learning methods, but question whether the students are truly engaged in their learning. What can you observe about the level of student engagement that might prove helpful to us to achieve full student engagement?

E. We have been working to increase the level of questioning and to set a goal with which half of teacher questions would be at a level of analyzing, evaluating, or creating outlined by Bloom's Revised Taxonomy. What evidence do you see that this is taking place?

F. Low-income students in our school perform significantly below the school and state averages. What evidence do you see for differentiated instruction for low-income students?

of problems of practice that a group could try ordering from least to most effective. These samples also include some limited school context information to sort through.

When the small groups are done, ask them to identify the problems they think are the weakest, say, those that rate either 1 or 2. Then ask them to identify those that are a bit better (3 and 4), before moving on to those ranked 5 and 6.

The key to this exercise involves asking groups to justify their evaluation of each problem of practice. Its purpose is to help them understand the criteria for a productive problem of practice. The participants may notice, for example, that A is not connected to the instructional core and that accurate data may be hard to obtain. B lacks targeted data about the problem and is therefore too general. C is more carefully defined but appears to assume that assignments are not part of the problem. E assumes a solution to a problem and represents an audit of teachers, not a true inquiry, and F is unobservable. D is the only statement that makes good use of data and is a true inquiry. In general, it's appropriate to rank E and F the lowest; A, B, and C toward the middle; and D the highest.

Strong Problems of Practice

You can then provide a final list of productive problems developed by a variety of past networks and ask the group to discuss the traits they share in common. Examples might include the following problems of practice:

- Is learning a mutual endeavor? Are the students who are sitting in groups helping each other learn? Do both teachers and students learn from each other?
- Are the students able to discuss concepts and content in the various subject areas?
- We would like to provide academic challenges for each child. What can you observe to help us accomplish this goal?

Each of these problems of practice represents a true inquiry in which the school asks for help from the visiting network, because it does not know what to do. In the preceding list, network observations are focused on learning as a mutual endeavor, students engaging in content discussion, and students being challenged. Consequently, the questions are derived from the instructional core, provide enough information to guide observations, focus on a problem of student learning, and are actionable by the school.

Why the Word *Problem*

The use of the word *problem* in a problem of practice sometimes bothers network members. The phrase is the subject of many comments, like, "Do we really want to use the word *problem*? That implies something negative, and what we are trying to do is positive. Wouldn't we be more accurate if we use *issues of practice*?"

I am resistant to using a word other than *problem* for several reasons. One aim of education is to learn to solve problems, which networks hopefully model through instructional rounds. Doctors have a problem of practice when a patient does not improve, and educators should have a problem when a student is not learning. Ask a doctor to explain her or his problem of practice, and you are likely to hear about a patient suffering complications from surgery or a puzzling condition, perhaps an unexpected allergic reaction. You go to doctors who are determined to solve health problems and take it as their professional responsibility to solve your problem. Ask an educator to explain her or his problem of practice, and too many complain about a reduced budget or the frustration of teaching kids with bad home lives or unmotivated students. These responses avoid responsibility.

Educators must take responsibility. If a teacher says, "I have a problem because I am unable to get every student to learn well," then we begin to identify the problem and take responsibility for solving it. It is not until we face our problems of finding ways to help all students learn well that we become more effective and accountable to results. The nature of a problem of practice is that it needs to focus on a problem of student learning.

VIDEO PRACTICE: OBSERVATION SKILLS

The third video is the group members' last opportunity to practice their observation skills together. Begin the network's third video observation by reminding the group that once again they will be observing classrooms at Friendly School around a problem of practice. The more authentically the simulation is constructed, the more likely the participants will be able to ask and address questions that accelerate learning. Ideally, this would mean using the first host school's problem of practice and offering the participants enough time to increase their knowledge about this issue. However, if the host school's problem of practice is not ready or well defined, you can use the Friendly School's hypothetical problem of practice about student engagement: "In what ways and to what extent are the students engaged in their learning?"

As you help them hone their observation techniques, it's important to tell them that while the problem of practice shouldn't guide their note taking too strictly, they should be aware of what are and aren't useful observations. Particularly when they are in the early stages of learning to use descriptive language, urge the participants to err on the side of taking more notes than less. However, such evidence as "saying the Pledge of Allegiance," or "a whiteboard is being used," or "one student talked to another," is not likely to shed light on the problem of practice, because the statements tell us little about the teaching or learning that is happening in the classroom. If a whiteboard is being used, we might want to know how and by whom—is it being used as a blackboard, or in some other way? If one student talked to another, we would want to know about what.

Just like the day before, you may decide to pause this video from time to time, depending upon your group and time constraints, again giving members time at the end to share what they saw and allowing them to check and compare notes with table-mates. You can sometimes appoint "evidence police" at each table to ask each person to share two pieces of evidence. In looking over their own observations, the members fine-tune their thinking on what descriptions are worthwhile to capture. Over time, the members discover that though they sometimes take fewer notes, the content is more purposeful. This is their last chance to practice with their colleagues before an actual school visit.

Choosing Videos

As mentioned in the discussion of the first launch day, facilitators should understand the importance of compatibility between the third video and the previous day's second video. For the purposes of simulation, these videos must share common traits of teaching and learning to enable members to find connections between the two when it is time to discern patterns of practice. If the classrooms in the videos depict very different teaching and learning roles, the members may become discouraged trying to discern patterns. Even though the two videos depict two different classrooms, together they must constitute a universe of classroom observation data that describe the instructional core at the fictitious Friendly School.

In selecting the two simulation videos, choose ones that model excellent classroom practices of high cognitive demand and student engagement, which then benchmark high standards of teaching and learning that network members can use when observing during rounds. On a side note, some participants in both the American and the Australian networks that I worked with expressed concern about whether the teachers featured in the TIMSS videos know how the videos are being used. When their concerns are expressed as questions like "Did this teacher agree to have his teaching picked apart like this?" it is clear that the videos offer a decided initial advantage for overcoming the culture of nice by launching forthright discussions of what is taking place in the classroom. But in answer to the question, the teachers and schools in the videos volunteered for the project, knowing that the videos would be viewed by educators around the world.

Homework

For the members who feel they need additional observation or note-taking practice, I recommend they observe the TIMSS videos available on the web, which are accompanied by printable transcripts if members wish to check their notes. Some members appreciate practicing in private early in their learning experience. Faculty members can also form pairs for observation practice in each other's or colleagues' classrooms. In these cases, the network members should clarify that it is for note-taking practice and their professional development and not for sharing or otherwise related to an analysis of teacher performance.

THE AFTERNOON: ANALYZING EVIDENCE AND FINDING PATTERNS

After the lunch break, the afternoon agenda is mostly devoted to having the network members learn how to debrief their observations in light of the problem of practice. This means they must select relevant evidence from their notes, screen and analyze the evidence, organize it into patterns, make predictions about the learning that should result from the teaching they observed, and then use this material to develop the next level of work for school improvement. Descriptions of each of these steps will be brief here, since the following chapters describe in greater detail the specific protocols used.

Simulation Debriefing

Before lunch, the small groups discussed their classroom observations. It is now time for them to select evidence from their notes—those they took during yesterday's second video and this morning's video. They will be looking over these notes to evaluate whether the notes constitute specific, objective, and informative data. This is a formal and challenging process that each member completes individually.

Members begin by sifting evidence from their many pages of notes, paper or electronic, on the two videos. Ask them to select pieces of evidence to enter onto sticky notes (one piece of evidence from a single classroom per one sticky note). The members may each generate five to ten sticky notes of evidence, or perhaps many more, per classroom. The evidence selected should be similar in form and quality to the specific and objective evidence sorted out on the previous day during the "From Observation to Evidence" exercise. The members each make their own pile of these sticky notes at their side in preparation for what comes next—evidence screening.

Once all members have filtered through their notes and transcribed selected notes as evidence on sticky notes, the facilitators lead the members through a screening protocol to vet the objectivity, specificity, and relevance of their evidence to the problem of practice. Generally the steps involved follow a team screening protocol, whose steps are briefly detailed in exhibit 4.4. (For a more thorough discussion of the team screening protocol, see chapter 6.)

From Screened Evidence to Developing Patterns

After the network members have screened all the sticky notes for solid evidence, they begin organizing them into patterns. The task here is to help the participants learn how to discern patterns of practice. In the case of the simulation, a pattern is formed when members find similar evidence occurring in both classroom videos, and it is related to the problem of practice. (This process is discussed in greater detail in chapter 7.)

EXHIBIT 4.4

The Team Screening Protocol for Screening Evidence

- Members sit in their small teams working as individuals to transcribe relevant observations onto sticky notes that they pile in front of themselves.

- Each member reads aloud his or her sticky notes to the small team.

- The small-team members screen every note as a group to be sure the notes are specific and objective.

- All notes that pass the small-team screening are placed at random on the chart or poster paper.

- Once placed on the paper, the results are owned by the entire small team.

To get started, it helps to discuss sample patterns. Examples might include these observations:

- Students sat in groups and worked individually.
- Teachers moved onto the next item upon one correct response.
- A select group of students answered all the teacher's questions.
- The content matched or exceeded grade-level standards.
- The students discussed content with each other before beginning to write.
- Teacher questions were recall and understanding.

It is often helpful to select at least one sample of poor quality and mark it in red to serve as a low benchmark. You then discuss the similarities and differences of the strong samples to make sure network members have a good idea of what they are expected to produce in the next step. High-quality patterns, like high-quality evidence, are specific and objective and provide information helpful to understanding the problem of practice. They communicate what the group of underlying evidence has in common and reveal as much as possible the extent of the evidence in the school. The network must always keep in mind that each pattern statement must stand on its own, leaving little room for misinterpretation or confused meaning. Each and every word must be well chosen.

The members begin by organizing evidence into groups that make sense to the team, summarizing each group with a descriptive statement similar in form to the samples just discussed. The table groups begin by organizing and reorganizing sticky notes in different configurations to discern patterns that shed light on aspects of the instructional core that support or hinder the resolution of the problem of practice at Friendly School: "In what ways and to what extent are students engaged in their learning?" The network must keep in mind that the question has been raised because the staff at Friendly School feel that student engagement is an important issue they would like to see improved. In this case, the network should fully explore all the factors that support or hinder full student engagement in this school.

Even though all the network members have viewed the same two videos, there will be considerable variation in the patterns developed by the different table groups. Some groups might find two patterns, while others may find seven. When multiple groups visit many classrooms in an actual rounds visit, there is significant variation in what is observed from one team to another, yet there is likely to be more similarity in patterns than the members anticipate. In the unlikely event that there is enough time, a discussion of the levels of Bloom's Revised Taxonomy or Costa's Levels of Thinking might be worthwhile at this juncture or put on the list as a potential in-service topic. As recommended in *Instructional Rounds*, these taxonomies, content standards, and other external frameworks are helpful to networks that are conducting an analysis of classroom observations. Another framework that is particularly helpful for the analysis of the instructional core and for application in the next level of work is "The Instructional Core Analysis Framework"(see appendix F).

Once each table group has completed patterns, the patterns are displayed with their accompanying evidence for a gallery walk. When all the groups have posted their patterns, each group reads them aloud one at a time to the network. The network's job is to assess whether the evidence supports, explains, and matches the descriptive statement. After each pattern is read, facilitators ask if further clarification is needed. When all the questions are answered to the network's satisfaction, the patterns are approved. The table groups in the live rounds sessions almost always need time during the group vetting process to search back through the evidence to revise or change their patterns in light of the vetting that takes place. The launch session may not have enough time for this, but it might be possible instead to have a brief discussion on revising patterns.

RECAP AND PREDICTIONS

After organizing their observation notes into patterns of practice, the members will now need to start connecting the patterns they have observed with what learning they would expect it to produce. In other words, in light of the patterns observed, what would you expect the students in this school to know and be able to do? This is the genesis of their predictions.

Instructional Rounds notes the prediction step often leads to collective "aha" moments and highlights the importance of detailed descriptive data as the basis for all conversation. As with much of rounds work, predictions can be completed in more than one way. The facilitator may begin by asking the network as a whole to offer predictions based on all of the patterns displayed. This is a good option if time is short. Facilitators may ask each small team to return to the tables to generate predictions based on the patterns written by the team. This work is then shared aloud, one group at a time, with the network.

Predictions, however, always address the same question: what would the students in this school know and be able to do in light of the patterns observed? Because this is the launch session, time will be short. Consequently, after the facilitator gives table groups a few minutes to discuss predictions, it is better to ask for samples from the group at large.

By connecting the dots from teaching and learning to the kind of student who will develop as a result, the process of making predictions should lead network learners to their next step, as described in the next section.

IMPLEMENTATION: THE NEXT LEVEL OF WORK

Once the network members have begun to tease apart what is happening in the classrooms, they can begin to formulate suggestions for what kinds of support or changes might help this school and district improve. This is the group's next level of work. The members of the network need to leave the launch session with a comprehensive idea of what they will be doing with the next level of work the next time they meet.

When deciding on the next level of work, the table groups should consider what the teachers and administration might do to move student engagement (Friendly School's problem of practice) to the next level. In the launch session, this work will be abbreviated because the videos limit observation data and are generated from a fictitious school with no context. Nevertheless, the members can still work on answering this question: given the patterns and predictions produced from the video work, what specific steps would the teams recommend to address the problem of practice, and what leadership and organizational practices are necessary to support this work at the school and district levels?

Once the teams generate ideas, they share them as the facilitator asks the teams to provide a rationale for what is recommended. The most useful suggestions for change are specific and concrete. It is easy to make general, vague suggestions, such as asserting that student learning would be better served with more academic assignments that demand critical thinking.

Deciding on the next level of work is not for the sake of a fictitious school. It is for network learning and preparation for the first school rounds session. Facilitators should take advantage of this opportunity to ask members to share what they learn from thinking through the next level of work, by asking, "How might this impact your own professional practice?" Detailed protocols for helping networks with the work of providing recommendations to host schools are covered in chapter 8.

DISCUSSING THE THEORY OF ACTION

Selection and enactment of recommendations issued in the next level of work demand a theory of action. The theory of action is a method to help leaders compare their planned actions for school improvement against what actually takes place over an extended period of time. This informs decision making as leaders formulate actions, make them known to those with whom they work, and test the effectiveness of declared actions using measures stipulated at the outset. We revise our thinking and decision making in light of experience, honing our leadership abilities according to results. The process is described in greater detail in chapter 9.

Team members are not asked to write a theory of action until they have gained enough experience in rounds and have enough collegial support to modify their personal goals with realistic expectations of what can be accomplished in one school year. Facilitators should nevertheless discuss the theory of action during the launch session to provide a long-term picture of how the participants will apply what they learn from rounds in professional practice. If time in the launch session is short, this presentation can be quite brief or even held off for another time. A facilitator can simply summarize the definition, purpose, and form of a theory of action.

The purpose of a theory of action is to make clear the relationship of essential elements of leadership to improved learning in the classroom in such a way as to enable tracking of learning over time. It should be an accurate representation of what you will do in your leadership role (teacher, principal, superintendent, network, etc.) to cause improved learning and to distinguish important elements of leadership action from those less important. It is an if-then proposition that captures the important connections between practice and what happens in classrooms. See exhibit 4.5 for a sample theory of action.

EXHIBIT 4.5

A Sample Theory of Action, School-Based

If I/we build instructional leadership through analyzing data, observing practice, and increased knowledge of the instructional core, then we will develop an informed and purposeful school improvement process that will lead to improved student learning.

PREPARING FOR A SCHOOL VISIT

At this point, as the afternoon begins to wind down, you are likely to be asked a number of questions about the upcoming school visit. Let's look at a few relevant questions.

What takes place as soon as we arrive at the host school?

A good time to discuss what takes place in the host school before classroom observations begin is just before viewing the last simulation video.

Their day begins at a host school as they gather in the library or another designated room and are greeted by the host principal, who shares a bit about the school's context and problem of practice. This is also a time to review the protocols for personal behavior during classroom visitations. These protocols are designed to establish safe and clear expectations about the network's presence in the school (see chapter 5).

I recall visiting a middle school in New Jersey, when a seventh-grade boy passed me in the hall and said, "Oh, you're one of the inspectors, aren't you?" This anecdote reveals much about the frame of reference teachers have for teams that visit schools. We know that rounds is different, but staff is less sure what to think. The network has to overcome a long history of teams visiting schools to rate and evaluate. Observation protocols are designed to help everyone overcome this.

It is helpful to warn against even innocent transgressions, like one observer's asking another observer for a pen—an action that the classroom teacher may interpret as distracting and rude. A casual comment made in the hallway about an experience elsewhere can be misinterpreted by passersby as an evaluation of what is currently happening in the host school. Members are not there to become part of the action, but to be as unobtrusive as possible.

Can additional nonnetwork host school staff be permitted to take part in rounds at their own school?

This should be a network decision. There are pros and cons to be weighed. It is helpful to the host principal and school for additional staff to see the objectivity and thoroughness of the network, understand firsthand that the network is trying hard to provide something of value to the school, and learn more about their own school by doing the work. It is also helpful for principals to have knowledgeable support when sharing rounds findings at the faculty meeting, adding to the credibility of events.

On the other hand, nonnetwork host staff members are not trained in observation techniques and did not take part in the development of norms. Some network members may legitimately feel uncomfortable and less free to share their observations if nonnetwork members are included. If nonnetwork members are included in one school, it may become common practice and permanently change the makeup and character of the network. The network must also consider the effects of a larger group and the addition of untrained members to small observation teams.

Facilitators should refer such requests to the think tank or to the network as a whole. This request sometimes arises at the last minute, too late for consideration by the network. In such circumstances, facilitators should feel free to say they are unable to authorize additional participants without the network's due consideration and permission.

Is the faculty on board? Will they know why we are there and what to expect when we enter the rooms? Will the students be willing to talk with us honestly?
The most productive problems of practice are developed with full faculty and staff input, which then implies tacit agreement about participating. The school has an inquiry stated in the problem of practice, and the network tries its best to shed light on the question by capturing an objective picture of what is taking place. Teachers need to know in advance the protocols of classroom observations as much as the network members need to live by them. There should be no surprises here.

As for the students, in all my years of doing rounds it is rare to find a student unwilling to talk. One of the great joys of rounds is talking with students of all ages. However, should a member find a student unwilling or uncomfortable, the member should move on to another.

How do we know the school is not putting on a show for us? Will we see a true picture of what usually goes on in the school? Or will the teachers prepare super lessons just for our visit?
If it truly wishes to benefit from a rounds visit, the school will not put on a staged event. This should be discussed with the entire network before school principals volunteer their schools as host. If the problem of practice is a true inquiry about a problem of student learning, then it is unlikely that a staged lesson will solve the problem. Likewise, if the school knows how to solve the problem of practice, a different problem should be used. We expect that teachers of host schools will do their

best teaching. However, it is helpful to think about the difference between doing one's best teaching and the ability to be a different kind of teacher from one day to the next.

For example, the first training video I often use demonstrates teaching in which students are asked low-cognitive-demand questions that require students to give one-word answers in less than two seconds. If no answer is forthcoming, the teacher calls on someone else or answers the question himself. What if such a teacher decided on the day of the rounds visit to stage a lesson in which he asked high-cognitive-demand questions and waited however long was necessary for the student to answer? The students would wonder what had happened to the teacher. It is sometimes easy to spot this in behavior that suggests that students are feeling, "Hey, what is going on here? I thought we had a deal. The teacher asks the questions, and if we don't answer immediately, the teacher asks someone else. If you don't put me on the spot, then I behave by minding my own business." The point is this: you can put on a good lesson, but the teacher-student roles are well established over time. The roles are impossible to change overnight.

There are other ways to test the authenticity of the teacher-student roles. If the observers believe that there are drastic differences in teacher and learner roles from one day to the next, more questions should be asked of the students. One suggestion is to ask students what they did in class the day before. Because it helps reveal the sequence of learning, the day-before question can be productive on its own.

Asking students, "Have you done this before?" can also be revealing. It may simply be that a large amount of practice work has been done or that the teacher is playing it safe by repeating a lesson that worked. Either way, what is being observed is a true reflection of what usually takes place in the classroom.

Another way to gain perspective is to ask the host school network members whether what they saw on the rounds visit rings true with what they would usually see. Again, the question should focus on the teacher-student roles, not on whether a whiteboard was used for the first time or whether the materials used in the lesson were specially prepared.

Is there an online tool on my tablet to tally observation data? Wouldn't it be better to use a camcorder to capture everything that goes on? Will I ever get better at note taking?

Those who ask about tallying observation data may come from a perspective of walk-throughs, in which a predetermined observation list of best practices is the basis for observation in classrooms. Rounds is descriptive and captures what currently exists in the interaction of the instructional core; it is quite different from a checklist or tally system. The school-generated problem of practice determines what evidence is most critical to capture from school to school. Instead of using a checklist or tally, the participants might try thinking of creative ways to organize their note taking to capture more interactions.

Camcorders sound like an attractive solution to solve the note taking dilemma, except for the steps involved in rounds. Camcorders capture lots of action, but what happens when you meet with colleagues to pull out evidence for analysis? You would need to replay the video to select evidence, thereby doubling the amount of observation time required. How would you interact with students if you were holding a camcorder? Would a camcorder be a distraction in the classroom?

Is there any proof that rounds increases test scores? Might it not be a better use of my time to work on raising test scores?

Rounds is not a test score improvement program. If the main interest is to improve test scores, you could use rounds as a vehicle to assist in that work. For example, you would analyze state test data and other indicators of student performance to identify an area of student learning problems. The problem of practice and consequently the observations captured would focus on the area identified. Rounds is intended for improving learning at scale, and learning at scale can only be accomplished through networks. It is up to the host school and network to derive as much benefit as possible from what is learned through rounds.

CLOSING EVENTS

This last portion of the agenda is important to facilitators and networks, as it is the last time you will see the network before visiting the first host school. Before you adjourn, take a few minutes to provide feedback on the last two days. You also need to recruit think tank volunteers, ask for member feedback on the two-day session, and hear from the next host school. This time should be preserved if necessary at the expense of extending work on other agenda items.

Working with Representatives of the First Host School

Hopefully, the first rounds visit will take place within the next three to four weeks, while what has been learned in the launch session is still fresh. To prepare, before this launch session is over, the network members need to hear from the leadership of the school to be visited. Both host schools and networks derive greater benefit from rounds when the network members know ahead of time something about the school context; the school's improvement efforts and school and student performance data; and why and how the problem of practice was selected.

This context is what the host school representatives should describe when they present their problem of practice. If the problem of practice is not yet fully developed, there will be time to discuss it again on the morning of the visit before the classroom observations occur.

The network also needs to know what the school hopes to gain from rounds. On the practical side, the host school representatives should provide a few details about parking, provision for lunch, where the members will convene, and so forth.

This is a good time to remind the host school representatives that the purpose of the upcoming rounds visit is primarily for the professional development of the members (including the school's own network participants) and the network even though it is hoped that the school will gain valuable insight and recommendations at the end of the rounds process. Be certain to connect with the host school representatives privately after the session but before they leave, to make sure that who does what, and when they do it, is agreed upon. Facilitators can also do this through e-mail if necessary, but doing so today may be helpful with lead time still available. As the launch session draws to a close, facilitators may take a few minutes for final questions. They might also assign homework, such as a reading assignment, further work finalizing a definition for something like student engagement, or the practice of observation skills with a suggested video on the Internet. There will be time to revisit all these issues in future rounds meetings.

Host School Volunteers

This is a good opportunity to ask the network's other principals to consider being additional host school volunteers. This early list enables the facilitator to work with the convening authority and perhaps the advisory council of think tank members (described below), to hammer out a schedule of host schools for the year and even into the next. Ideally, the facilitator will be releasing this schedule as early as the second rounds session to give the network members time to mentally prepare.

Candidates for the Think Tank

The end of the launch session is the best opportunity to recruit interested volunteers for the think tank. You can start by reminding the network that rounds work is developmental. Its long-term goal is for the network to eventually assume responsibility for its own learning. Explain that the think tank will become increasingly critical as a kind of advisory body, as the facilitator's leadership becomes less and less necessary. Tell them that as a long-term guiding council of not much bigger than six to eight (depending on the size of the network), think tank members meet occasionally outside of network sessions to discuss network progress, in person, over the phone, or by e-mail. Their duties include providing advice and feedback; planning agendas; and acting as a liaison between the facilitator and the network, the facilitator and the district, and even between the network members themselves. They discuss issues of network functioning, host school schedules, in-service topics, and implementation of the work. They oversee how learning and implementation are progressing, and consider complaints or conflicts. The network received a taste of think tank duties with the ad hoc think tank that helped finalize the group's norms. (For this short-term duty, volunteers worked through lunch or at the close of the first day or before the beginning of the second day of the launch session. It gave them a bit of authentic work and a sense of the think tank's role in relation to the network.)

More Feedback

Be sure to collect the session feedback surveys before the participants depart (exhibit 4.6). The surveys take five to ten minutes to complete and provide anonymous

---

EXHIBIT 4.6

Launch Session Feedback Questions

1. What was your experience like as a learner these past two days?
2. What insights, if any, have you gained about teaching and learning?
3. What kind of learning worked best for you? When were you the most alert or challenged?
4. What did the facilitator(s) do that contributed to your experience?
5. What could the facilitator(s) do to help your learning in the future?
6. What are the implications for your own work, and did you discover an idea, a practice, or some other technique you might try?
7. Do you have any other comments or lingering questions?

feedback of enormous value that enable facilitators to hone their own skills and gauge network development and next steps to take. You contribute to network development by sharing the results of these surveys to help members learn how their colleagues have responded to rounds work.

It can help members feel less isolated in their struggle with the material to hear their colleagues say, "The material is inspiring, but daunting. There's so much to learn," or "I'm feeling overwhelmed by the steep learning curve. There are so many variables that go into teaching and learning practices that we have not even touched upon. It's so complicated," or "It's eye-opening to look at teaching and learning through student output."

Likewise, objective, specific feedback from the facilitator about the network's growth, development, and issues of concern demonstrates and models productive teaching and learning. Such feedback encourages the network to use the session feedback forms thoughtfully at future sessions.

Openly sharing experiences builds collegiality, while encouraging members to consider these reflections as empowerment opportunities for possible action. Having these thoughts on the table allows for discussion and enables facilitators to assist if needed. (The think tank also serves this purpose by encouraging its network colleagues to share their reflections on rounds work and integrate this learning into more systemic professional practice.)

Closing Launch Session Remarks

Facilitators should assume that rounds work is new to members. Even seemingly unimportant pieces of the agenda can add to the complexity and overwhelm members. When facilitators in one launch session revealed that a high school would serve as the first host school, the members wondered aloud whether they were equal to the task. A show of hands from this preK–12 network revealed that for the majority, this would be their first return to high school classrooms since they were teens. The same level of concern is often true of high school staff visiting elementary classrooms. It is helpful for members to see they are not alone.

Facilitators should encourage members to keep a journal for their own personal use in which they can note unanswered questions and items to improve their practice. There is often a month or more between rounds visits, and if a participant doesn't write down his or her thoughts, learning can be interrupted, if not forgotten.

Over the two-day launch session, you will see the network participants grow in confidence, which only increases over the succeeding rounds sessions. Most participants don't really feel up to speed until they have about three or four rounds sessions behind them. This will happen to your network, but not just because they have more practice. It is due to the constructivist and developmental nature of instructional rounds itself. Instructional rounds, a well-designed and highly successful route to school improvement, is being implemented productively by many thousands of educators across the globe. There is no reason to suspect that your network will be any different.

PART 3

Facilitating School Rounds Visits

CHAPTER 5

Preparing to Observe

School rounds visits are highly scheduled affairs. They need to run like clockwork, although they often don't. Besides having to adhere to a strict schedule, network members need to concentrate on gathering objective observations and follow carefully constructed protocols. There are multiple reasons for these protocols and asking network members to be self-conscious about their presence. For the school's sake, as well as for the integrity of the rounds process, it is important that they not disrupt or otherwise change classroom dynamics or wrongly be perceived as evaluating and therefore be misunderstood.

Your job as facilitator, on the other hand, is a bit like being a ringmaster for the day. You introduce and manage the process, juggle the time to allow for completion of the most critical activities, ensure that arrangements are followed on all sides, attend classroom visits, and, at the end, become the network's liaison to the school and the district when the results are ready to be conveyed.

The learning objectives for these visits are threefold and help to further nearly all the network goals: (1) to strengthen a shared culture and practice through building relationships based on inquiry, trust, candor, and support; (2) to continue to deepen a shared understanding of the instructional core through authentic experience; and (3) to learn to use rounds individually and collectively to improve student learning.

OVERVIEW OF THE ROUNDS VISIT

School rounds visits follow the same procedures—of observation and description before analysis, analysis before prediction, and prediction before formulation of the next level of work—whether you are visiting your first host school or last as well as whether you are visiting for one day or a day and a half. (Sometimes, networks conduct the entire rounds visit process in one day. It becomes rushed, the next level of work gets neglected, and there is not time to pursue questions for additional in-service sessions. For these reasons, I don't recommend this shortened schedule.)

Let's start by looking at an overview of the entire rounds visit. Exhibit 5.1 outlines this agenda.

This chapter will cover only the first morning of a school rounds visit—the pre-observation meeting and the classroom visits themselves. It will discuss some of the most common questions, comments, and concerns generated by the network members during these morning activities. The remainder of the first day's work and that of the next day will be covered in subsequent chapters. While the rounds process—observations, analysis of evidence, predictions about what students in the school should know and be able to do, and recommendations about the school's next level of work—can be completed more quickly and smoothly by experienced network teams, these activities are complex and involve definite protocols and a number of formal steps. That is why the complex details of the remainder of the rounds school visit, the afternoon and morning of the next day, will be discussed over the next several chapters.

THE MORNING: PREOBSERVATION MEETING

Schedule network rounds visits for as full a day as the union contract allows, preferably an 8 a.m. to 4 p.m. school day (and one-half day the following day). Facilitators should plan on arriving at least a half hour early to take care of essentials. A room should have already been set aside for the network and should ensure the privacy of conversations and security of written material and personal belongings. This room, often the library, should be checked to ensure that the relevant technology is in place, that everyone's place around the tables has the necessary materials, that poster material is on hand, and so on. Your list of team assignments may need adjusting if members are missing. The materials list is essentially the same as that for the launch session (see exhibit 3.2).

Review of Principal's Remarks

Before the network members arrive, the facilitator should meet with the host school principal to review his or her opening presentation to the network. This way, the

---

EXHIBIT 5.1

Agenda for 1½-Day Rounds Visit

First Day

8:00–9:00	Greetings, introduction to school, preobservation meeting
9:00–10:20	Classroom observations (four 20-minute periods)
10:20–10:30	Break
10:30–12:00	Debrief observations and screen evidence
12:00–12:45	Lunch
12:45–2:30	Develop and vet patterns
2:30–2:45	Break
2:45–3:15	Revise patterns, make predictions
3:15–3:45	Reflections on the day, and adjournment

Second Day (Morning Only)

8:30–8:45	Greetings, interim feedback from host school
8:45–9:30	Follow-up in-service on questions of interest to network
9:30–10:30	Develop next level of work, including brief discussion of host school resources to address the problem of practice, the faculty sharing protocol, the strategic starting point protocol, and completion of the next level of work
10:30–10:45	Break
10:45–11:30	Teams present next level of work, questions from host school
11:30–11:40	Host school feedback to the network
11:40–11:50	Discussion with the next school to host rounds visit
11:50–12:00	Reflections from members
12:00–12:15	Session feedback process, facilitator observations, adjourn
12:15–12:45	Facilitator meets privately with host school and central office to support implementation work; release of network findings to take place as soon as possible

facilitator can make sure that the principal is still on the same page with the original understanding of the context and the problem of practice. The principal may need to adjust the schedule of the network teams' classroom assignments. Sometimes, changes must be made if teachers are absent and substitutes have taken over a classroom slated for a visit. Substitute teachers obviously do not represent the ongoing professional practice of the school, and visiting their rooms would undermine all data. But substantial changes to the visit schedule or the problem of practice are unacceptable. Too many people have invested too much in this visit to allow for changes that jeopardize the value of the visit.

Sometimes, however, even after you have discussed the visit and helped the host school develop a workable problem of practice and classroom visit schedule, you arrive the morning of the visit only to discover that the classroom schedule or problem of practice, or both, have been changed and redone in such a way as to compromise the value of the visit. This happened to me once when the host principal of a 1,500-student high school handed the thirty-four-member network a classroom schedule that limited us to a total of eight classrooms in the school. The team members were stunned. The host principal was even a member of the network that had participated in prior rounds visits. It was too late to change the schedule, so the entire group of eight network teams visited a total of eight classrooms, selected from one wing of the entire school. The results from such a tightly scheduled visit are likely to be viewed by the larger school faculty as representative of the teaching and learning in those eight classrooms only, and therefore viewed by the rest of the faculty as irrelevant to school-wide practice. Such a visit has limited application and impact. While there are occasions when a host school and network could decide intentionally to focus on one small group of classrooms, such a decision should reflect the problem of practice, shared goals, and collective discussion. In the case of the aforementioned school, the problem of practice inquired about school-wide issues, and these could not be addressed with the change in schedule. To this day, I am still dumbfounded by what happened, but the event led me to change my facilitation practices. There are many surprises you will encounter and can tolerate; this is one you can't.

Always carefully review the final copy of the schedule from the school in advance. The transmission of this information and your consequent confirmation must establish this as the final document. Make this clear. You are responsible not just for your time in carefully choreographing the day; you are also responsible for the valuable time of your entire network. Facilitators should expect the life of a principal to be hectic or that all kinds of things come up, or that the work can get delegated to someone unaware of the intricate nature of the schedule. You should expect this and, with the host principal, forge an agreement that no changes will occur without your knowledge well in advance. This means you must insist on absolute clarity around a firmly cast schedule and problem of practice prior to the day of the visit.

Arrival of Network Members

As network members convene at the host school, there is usually great anticipation. The day has finally come to put into practice what they have learned. Again they gather around coffee and baked goods. Copies of the schedule and maps of the school's floor plan are placed before chairs at the tables along with other meeting supplies.

The Schedule Details

The schedules detail the members' team assignments, classroom numbers, and teachers' names to eliminate confusion. The problem of practice is noted right on the schedule. These schedules deliberately omit specific time for passing between classrooms. This is to discourage hallway conversation about visits before the members have had an opportunity to digest what they have seen. Hallway wait time also invites conversation that is easily misinterpreted by the passing host staff, and rumors fly quickly in schools. For another look at the team and classroom assignment schedule, see exhibit 2.2.

Convening the Network and Making Opening Remarks

The facilitator opens the day with introductory remarks that remind the network members that even though an important objective of their work over the next two days and beyond is to help the school solve its problem of practice, the members are not yet in command of conducting the rounds process or enacting what they learn through rounds to improve their professional practice. Particularly for the first several rounds visits, rounds is first and foremost about network learning. After this visit and on subsequent rounds visits, it is likely that the members will strategize how to do things more effectively from one rounds to the next, so keeping a journal will ensure they don't forget their problems to overcome, improvement ideas, and questions to ask in later sessions. The next rounds visit is likely to be a month away, and without notes, such thoughts may be lost.

The facilitator should again review the protocols for visiting classrooms, reminding the team members to refrain from talking with other team members in classrooms and hallways and to turn off all electronic communications. Statements of network norms should be left on each table beside schedules and supplies. See exhibit 5.2 for a list of visit protocols.

Also in the opening remarks, remind the members to concentrate on capturing the full interactions of the instructional core. Explain that it is better to have descriptive, detailed notes of specific interactions than to try to cover everything that is going on in the classroom.

The Importance of Destroying Observation Sticky Notes

As final advice, it's usually a good idea to remind the members that their observation notes are their property for private use and that the sticky notes will be destroyed after the work is completed. While practice among experienced rounds facilitators does vary, I have found that releasing sticky notes—which identify individual classrooms, teachers, and, possibly, students—can become a distraction and can lead to the work's being misunderstood. Faculty can become defensive, and the all-important school-wide patterns the network has worked so hard to unearth can get lost in the process. Only work that has been vetted and approved by the network, establishing network standards and ownership of the work's quality, is forwarded to the school.

EXHIBIT 5.2

Observation Protocols

- Visits are twenty minutes per classroom (four classrooms).
- Silence electronic devices.
- Enter (without knocking) and leave as a group.
- Arrive with note paper and pen (or substitute).
- Refrain from acknowledging teacher or class upon entering or leaving.
- Go to seating, if it is provided, or sit off to the side.
- Move about room, and talk to students when appropriate.
- Refrain from talking to network colleagues in class or hall.

Principal's Introduction of School Context

Host principals present the school's educational context—what the school is trying to accomplish, the problem of practice, and relevant school pedagogical issues, demographics, or other items of special interest related to the problem of practice. This information helps orient network members as they begin to focus on the problem of practice in classrooms. Allow your network a few minutes to ask the principal questions, such as what kinds of notes might be particularly helpful to the school. Make sure the participants have a clear understanding of the problem of practice. This preobservation time is their final few moments to be clear about the authentic circumstances of the classroom and school before they enter the classrooms.

Strategizing the Visits

Before leaving for their designated classrooms, each team of three to four members will need to decide how they will go about managing classroom observations. Give them about ten minutes for this process. Since there are several issues for them to discuss, each team should appoint a scribe to report its decisions to the group. The teams need to establish observation strategies that specify how they will jointly cover the classroom, which observations about the teacher and student in the presence of content would yield the most helpful evidence to the host school in exploring the problem of practice, and what questions they might ask students.

Deciding on Where to Look, What to See

Solving these issues is difficult for many members. Stressed about their observational work, some members feel awkward and don't know where to focus as they enter the room. This is why the teams need to consider these issues before they arise. If members intend to talk with students, the team might decide to separately cover different parts of the classroom to do so. If students are working in groups, the members might decide to divide themselves between the groups, staying with one or floating between them. If the team is interviewing students about their work, the members might agree to talk with students about different topics so that a team member doesn't repeat the same conversation if the same student happens to talk with more than one team member. Facilitators ask the teams to share aloud their preliminary planning so that the entire network can revise strategies in light of the ideas offered by colleague teams. Well-thought-out ways to share observation practice enables for a more comprehensive evidence base and more productive team analysis.

Facilitators on Observation Teams

When the members depart for classroom visits with their schedule in hand, each cofacilitator, or single facilitator, joins a team, perhaps filling in where a member is absent or a team is undersized. Facilitators will find this informative to their work. They can assess how the teams travel throughout the building, can model observation behaviors, and can observe the teaching and learning in classrooms that will be discussed over the remainder of the session. Facilitators may choose to visit all four classrooms or only three out of the four in order to return to the meeting room early, ahead of the network to prepare for the next stage of work. What facilitators do with their observation notes will be discussed in the next chapter.

THE MORNING: CLASSROOM VISITS

As the network observation teams stand, anxious to be on their way and armed with maps, schedules, pens, and paper to start their visits, the school day has already begun. You may need to hold an avid group back so that a classroom is not entered before the schedule calls for it. If a team member cannot keep up with the team, the team should pause, so that everyone can enter the classroom together. Tell your team that to minimize classroom disruption, observers should not separately enter classrooms one at a time.

In classrooms around the school, lunch counts and attendance have been taken, morning announcements have concluded, and lessons have begun. Your rounds classroom visits are purposely timed in such a way that the network members can take advantage of their observation time to focus data gathering on interactions pertinent to the problem of practice.

As the teams scatter throughout the building to the first of their four assigned classrooms, they arrive at classroom doors and enter without knocking, quietly as a team. They should survey the room and either go immediately to the chairs set aside for them or, if there are no chairs, move to the side to orient themselves to what is going on in the lesson. This is a good time for the members to jot down such information as the grade level or subject area of the classroom they are in, the count of students by gender, seating configuration, and assignments displayed by the teacher as a part of initial observations. After a few minutes, they should know whether they can circulate quietly around the room to study student work and to interview students. Hopefully, the lesson isn't one in which the teacher does all the talking and is simply addressing the class. When students are required to sit quietly, listening to the teacher, the observation team may be forced to sit tight and just listen in, rather than wander around the room and talk to the students. Regardless, the team should be taking notes as casually and unobtrusively as possible.

The members will need to keep an eye on the time to depart after twenty minutes for their next class. They won't have time to linger and should leave together quietly. When arriving at the next class, the first team may not yet have vacated the classroom. The arriving team should not hesitate to enter the room (in silence) despite the presence of the other team. It is better for the arriving team to enter than to stand outside in the hallway. No doubt, the lingering team members will realize immediately that they have delayed beyond their time and must now move on to their next classroom. In light of the tightness of the day's agenda, the network members will need to immediately reconvene in the meeting room after their fourth and final class, to begin their next phase of work.

INSIDE THE CLASSROOM: QUESTIONS AND CONCERNS

Over the years, I have heard from many network members about issues that arise during classroom visits. I hear many of the same concerns over and over. Here are some of the challenges raised.

Not Enough Observation Time

Don't be surprised by network members who question whether twenty minutes (or even twenty-five) is long enough to get a solid sense of what is going on in a classroom. Many participants ask to lengthen classroom visits, complaining that such short viewing time makes them uncomfortable. This concern has been expressed by a member or two in nearly every network I've worked with. Observers worry they just don't have enough time to understand very much about what is taking place, but it is also an interesting coincidence that most union contracts require that formal evaluation visits be longer than twenty minutes to enable teachers a fair opportunity to demonstrate their professional abilities.

I have learned not to debate with networks about this. Instead I ask that they take a wait-and-see approach and revisit the question after they have made a few more rounds visits.

In the meantime, it is helpful to remind members of a few things: the object of each visit is to take a sample of multiple teacher-student interactions to ascertain teaching and learning patterns across the school. With two teams visiting every classroom, samples are being gathered by multiple members across multiple grades and multiple subject areas, which in aggregate provides a fairly comprehensive and representative picture. The purpose, after all, is to understand the cause and effect of a teaching and learning practice, not to evaluative individuals.

Facilitators can also note (and should note at some point) that a schedule for eight observation teams results in a total of sixteen different classrooms being observed. Each classroom is observed twice, resulting in a total of thirty-two classroom observation sessions of twenty minutes each. If each team has four members producing a set of notes for each classroom observation session, the process yields 128 sets of individual classroom observation notes—a very large volume of detailed data indeed.

Dividing Observation of the Instructional Core Among Team Members

Many team members fear missing an important piece of action in the classroom. Concern about this impels team after team to brainstorm ways to ensure that their observation notes are truly comprehensive. This leads many teams to the same solution: something I call the division-of-labor approach. If this idea doesn't come up in the first rounds, it often does in the second or third. It begins with someone proposing that the most efficient way to take notes would be for one person to take notes on the teacher; another on the students; yet another on the assignments, tasks, and wall displays; with the last team member asking students questions.

It is great that network members are struggling to be as thorough as possible, and while this approach might make note taking easier, it limits understanding of what is actually taking place in the classroom. Try to reassure the team members that it isn't possible or even necessary that each person capture everything in their notes.

Members should keep in mind that dividing observation responsibilities in this way leads to notes that reflect division of the three pieces of the instructional core, while it is actually the interactions between teacher, student, and content that are more important. Most of the advice in this book emphasizes the value of capturing as much as possible the full interaction of the instructional core, even if it means ignoring other classroom events to complete noting down one revealing interaction.

It's helpful to remind observers that by dividing the instructional core, crucial information will be missing. For instance, it is often not possible to determine the cognitive level embedded in a teacher's question without connecting it directly to the student's response, the level of content in relation to the student's knowledge, or how the teacher reacts to the student's response. A question that may appear to be of high cognitive demand might be nothing more than a question answered by recall of content from the day before. In a similar manner, wall displays or what is written on the board are of no value until we discover, by talking to the students or observing their work, whether the students are using the displayed content. If not, such displays are nothing more than decoration.

What Kind of Observation Data Best Informs the Problem of Practice?

This question is a continual challenge for observers, but especially difficult for those new to rounds and who have no experience observing with a problem of practice in mind. Network members often talk about the pressure they feel, not only to come up with observations that are specific and objective, but also to come up with a description that is valuable and relevant to the school's stated problem of practice.

It may help if they took a few moments before beginning their observations by imagining what the instructional core might look like if the school's particular problem of practice were resolved. For example, if the problem of practice had to do with rigorous learning in connection with higher-order thinking skills, what might teachers and students be doing and saying? What would the level, complexity, and role of content look like? Likewise, what might observers see and hear if the core lacked the rigor of cognitive demand? These extreme two images may help clue members into the range of what they should be collecting information on in the classrooms they visit.

Too Narrow a Focus on the Problem of Practice

Members eager to be helpful can get trapped into thinking a problem of practice should define all their observations. Focusing observations too narrowly on what is thought to be the problem of practice can be like taking notes with blinders on. Particularly at the beginning of the rounds process, it can be difficult to discern what is relevant in the midst of the demands of a classroom setting. Being more relaxed about recording what is happening and sorting it out later captures a fuller picture and is better than beginning observations with a filter that could miss what might later be recognized as relevant. Notes that were considered only tangentially related to the problem of practice when they were taken are often later discovered to be highly useful.

Take for example, a problem of practice on student engagement. A member may interpret student engagement to be students working hard on what the teacher asked them to do—a restrictive definition that may be reflected in their team discussion and observation strategies, and therefore might limit their note taking. In this case, members sometimes return with very few notes from a classroom observation, and when I ask them how it went, they reply, "I was looking for student engagement, but didn't see much, so I don't have many notes."

A lot of evidence, like "The teacher called on a student with her hand up," or "A student asked whether the teacher wanted the class to complete all the examples," or "One student asked another for help and was told the answer, " does tell us something about teaching and learning in the classroom. These notes are informative about problems of practice like student engagement, the role students play in assessment, who does the work, and cognitive demand. With observation-note evidence like these examples, the role of students in these classrooms becomes clearer, and useful information about the school's problem of practice is revealed.

The balance between notes that draw a rich description of all interactions and those that narrowly focus on the problem of practice is a difficult one to achieve. Only when the group is uncovering patterns might it realize that some helpful description might be missing. It is better to capture more evidence and let extraneous evidence go unused during the debriefing. Facilitators should urge rich, objective descriptions of interactions by noting that it is not until the evidence is reviewed that a determination of relevance or importance is revealed.

The Kinds of Questions to Ask Students

Another question I get asked all the time is about the many kinds of questions to ask students. The problem of practice might require members to get a picture of how students regard their roles as learners, or whether students have a conceptual understanding of the content of what they're doing, or whether students find the task challenging, or how students know they have produced good work. Network members should develop specific questions before entering the classroom.

There are probably as many questions as there are problems of practice, but the problem of practice should serve as the questioner's general guide. It can help in deciding what questions to ask students so that the answers illuminate something about the problem of practice.

Using Questions to Clarify What Is Going On

Observers might also use questions to help them sort out what they are seeing in the classroom. For example, an observer might be confused about what the teacher is saying. By asking students, observers might get clarification, while also receiving insight into student understanding of the task. These kinds of answers might include: "We started this yesterday, so she is just reminding us about what comes next," or "You've got me. I have no clue," or "She wants us to explain why we think the Colonialists threw the tea in the Boston harbor." Although students tend to be excellent and reliable sources, observers should know that it might be helpful to query several students to keep atypical responses in perspective.

Some questions are tied directly to classroom events, while others are more methodical, preselected queries that are asked of many students in multiple classrooms. This is a way to develop a database of responses to questions related to the problem of practice. If the problem of practice is about whether students are challenged in their thinking, a team might decide to ask multiple students in every classroom whether they find the work challenging or easy. But if this is part of a team's plan, the team could return quite disappointed when it has no chance to ask them. Members need to plan on a variety of strategies to explore the problem of practice every time they visit a classroom to get a comprehensive picture.

Facilitators should encourage thinking through the subtle differences in how questions are worded. For example, "What are you learning?" is quite different from "What are you learning about?" The first question asks about new knowledge the student is acquiring. The second may only reveal the topic of the lesson without tapping into whether the student is actually learning something new or of consequence.

Using Follow-Up Questions to Complete the Picture

Often it is the follow-up question that is the more informative. For example, when I was quizzing a fourth-grade student who had been given twenty dollars in play money for purchases in which to make change, she told me the work was easy. When I asked her what made it easy, she said she had done the same thing last year in third grade. So I asked if she would like the work to be harder. She said, sure, because now that she was in fourth grade, she should have at least forty dollars. In this way, she was communicating beyond doubt what she thought of the work she was doing.

In another example, an eighth-grader described his work as challenging because he had to answer many questions in a short amount of time. He then added that the questions weren't all that hard, because all the answers were in the notes. In this case, the student's definition of challenge referred to the amount of work, not its intellectual rigor. This is important particularly if the problem of practice is about the intellectual challenge experienced by students. Facilitators should remind participants to always probe beneath the surface when asking questions.

Another issue of note is to remind members to be aware of the fine line between recording word for word what a student says and interpreting what the student says. Follow-up questions clarifying the meaning of the student's answer can resolve such dilemmas. Facilitators should discuss the practice of asking follow-up questions and point out when members use them well. Regarding quotes, it makes a member's observation notes more useful if quotation marks are used to differentiate the quoted answer from a paraphrase.

The takeaway here is that facilitators help network members enormously by giving teams some minutes before they depart for classroom visits to discuss what questions they might ask students in light of the school's problem of practice.

Distrusting What Students Say

Some members are skeptical about using what they are told by students when they are looking at teaching and learning. Some participants have difficulty trusting student answers as honest or reliable. When questions are not asked, however, some portion of an important element of the instructional core (the student) will be missing and deny network members a valuable source of analysis.

There may be reason to distrust what students say to teachers when a teacher's role is to maintain discipline and a student's is to be compliant and follow directions while waiting to be filled with knowledge. Ironically, research tells us that students are more reliable than teachers in reporting what takes place in the classroom. Students have been shown to be reasonably accurate appraisers of a teacher's ability to help them learn.

Thus, facilitators should encourage members to be open to seeking student input and to observe student work. We focus on what students make, do, say, or write because it is the true accountability of learning. In order to improve student learning, we need to know what students think about what they are learning and why. The facilitator's role is not to convince members of the value of what students tell them. It is to encourage members to develop effective questioning techniques and to ask the all-important follow-up questions so that members can decide for themselves whether to trust what the students tell them. Facilitators should definitely use the preobservation session to explore these issues.

One joy of participating in rounds is talking with students and asking them questions. The students are likely to view the network members as independent of the school's student-teacher relationships and respond quite honestly, sometimes more than you would like to hear.

Asking Teams to Summarize Their Strategy Decisions

After allowing for these discussions in the preobservation meeting, facilitators should ask team representatives one at a time to provide highlights of their discussions, including specifics on the kind of notes and questions they have decided to pursue. Teams should expect to justify their thinking to the group. Upon conclusion of team sharing, allow a few minutes for the teams to adjust their strategies in response.

The purpose here is not to develop perfect strategies or ideal questions. An experienced facilitator learns to encourage the members to try things out, despite seeing flaws in their strategies, ideas, or questions. The session is designed to support a culture of safe risk-taking among colleagues. Colleagues take risks when exchanging ideas within their team and should feel empowered to explore strategies without being certain how well they'll work out. The risk of emotional exposure when reporting to the network is buffered by responding as a team, while the entire network benefits by hearing new ideas and strategies—another way to develop shared practice.

As they walk around this brain-storming session, facilitators should take notes about what issues were discussed within the teams and how many and what type of revisions were made after network sharing. This is good material for determining progress and reinforcing the power of risk-taking and shared practice, something you should offer as feedback to the network on their progress.

This session's purpose is also to hone strategizing skills. The teams record their strategies and are asked, after observing, how well their strategies worked and whether they might do something differently next time. The only way to learn how to do this work is to do the work.

THE FIRST SCHOOL HOSTS: NETWORK TRIAL BALLOONS

Your early classroom rounds visits are all about network trust. It is important that they go well, since they can establish network attitudes and feelings about a process that may include the participants' own schools. In a sense, the first couple of visits set up the following visits as network members appraise how much they can trust the network process and each other. The first rounds visit establishes the way the rounds process works. It therefore should be as good an example as possible for clarifying the work for members considering how they may feel about hosting a rounds visit at their own school. How the work is accomplished between facilitator, network, and host school may determine whether other schools volunteer to host in the future.

The members will want to see whether support was in fact given to the host school throughout the process; whether the host school's interests were honored; whether the host school had a sense that it had control over developing important parts of the process, like the writing of the problem of practice; and whether the host school got the kind of help and support it needed for this task. The first and second schools serve as a kind of a trial balloon for other potential host school volunteers.

A WORD OF ENCOURAGEMENT

Despite all this nervous chatter and stress about trying to follow observation protocols, once nerves have calmed and network members get a few rounds visits under their belt, the members find the work rewarding, fascinating, and fun—and, eventually, not all that stressful. The work nonetheless will be increasingly challenging as members become more skilled in the observation process: in other words, the more insightful the observations and the better the notes, the more complex and comprehensive the debriefing.

CHAPTER 6

From Observation to Evidence

Upon returning from their classroom visits (around 10:30), network members appreciate a few minutes to chat and gather their thoughts over refreshments. This is also a time for them to review notes while their observations are still fresh in their memories. This gives facilitators the opportunity to check in with the host school members since many are often anxious about having their school under scrutiny. It is a new experience for them to join their network colleagues on an observational tour of their own classrooms, and to do it in order to gather objective evidence is a very, very different way of looking at the familiar.

During one of my assignments, one dedicated Australian principal returned downcast from a network visit to his school. "I'm discouraged," Anthony said, noting he'd hoped to see something different from the uninspiring scenes he and his rounds team had just viewed in his classrooms. "I know there are lots of good things going on at my school, but now I see we have much work to do," he said. "It's depressing."

In talking to discouraged participants like this principal, you have the opportunity to both reassure and nudge them toward change by helping them use their discouragement as a motivator for productive action. Reassure them that their training in objective observation has helped them better understand the teaching and learning in their school. The question is what they plan to do with it. You can assure them that the painful clarity of this moment is what many principals of host schools feel. Remind them that the network's observations will soon provide them the data they needed to help pinpoint and address the problems in their classroom practice. And, membership in the network, you can add, will assure them the support they would need to get there.

PROCESSING EVIDENCE

This chapter covers how network members process their observation notes once they return from the classrooms. I have discovered the hard way that the only way to take this raw evidence and turn it into the honed data that provides a clear, objective portrait of the school's instructional core is through a careful reviewing and screening process structured by rather strict protocols. This chapter is about that process and those protocols. The following chapters will describe what to do with the data once it is screened.

WARM-UP: DISCUSSING AND REVIEWING THE OBSERVATION VISIT

Once the midmorning break is over and everyone is ready to work, start by asking the network for general feedback on how well their team observation strategies worked—which strategies succeeded, which didn't, what warranted change, and what approaches should be eliminated. If comments do not come forth immediately, you should wait. This is a significant step, the network's first serious discussion about the experience of devising and executing observation strategies to collect useful evidence.

Members' Perceived Problems with Observation Experiences in the Classroom

Eventually participants begin to speak up, often making these kinds of statements:

- "We only had time to ask a few questions from our long list. I don't think we have very much information about any one question."
- "We didn't plan on the students working at interest centers. I don't have very many notes."
- "I realize now that my notes are almost exclusively about the teacher. Our plan to spread out our attention would have worked better had I stuck to it."
- "One of our classes was in Spanish, and I don't speak Spanish."

In response to these problems, a facilitator could then ask for suggestions about what the participants might want to do differently next time or whether anyone could offer suggestions about how to approach such problems in the future. The focus at this point is to guide the group to use a model of shared problem-solving and shared practice. Members should be given a few moments to reassess their observation strategies and make journal entries about what they think could improve these observation skills on their visit to the next school.

Discussing the Complexities of Talking to Students

The next step is to move the group to discuss what they observed. You can jump-start the conversation by soliciting samples of observations organized according to grade level, by visitation team, by elements of the instructional core, or through items related to the problem of practice. Lots of interesting material is generated in these general discussions.

Here is one example of the kind of evidence you're encouraging network members to look for. The observation team of a group that I was facilitating happened to include the host principal. We observed a first-grade classroom centered on the teaching of learning intentions. The first-graders were all wearing file cards hung on yarn around their necks. Each card stated a learning goal in a sentence that began "My learning goal is . . ." and ended with a learning goal, different for each student and written in hand on the card by the teacher.

The host principal reported to the network that when he knelt beside one little girl's desk to ask about her learning goal ("to make little words out of big words"), the girl was able to state what the teacher had written.

Impressed, he asked, "Well, can you tell me a big word?"

"Yes," said the girl. "Cat."

Not sure what to think, he went a bit further: "Can you tell me a little word that comes from *cat*?"

"Of course," she responded. "Kitten."

Whether this report truly happened as described or is just an embellished recollection, it exemplifies the importance of going one step further. With these first-grade students able to state their learning goals, the classroom visitor could have left it at that. But in taking his investigation a step further by interviewing the students, he'd learned he'd have to adjust his expectations about what was happening in the lesson. Only by querying one of the students about her understanding of her goal did he learn that her interpretation differed from the learning intention expressed by the teacher. The takeaway, of course, is that we know little about student understanding without asking the students directly. We do not know what is taking place with teaching and learning without observing and talking with students.

As the network discusses the experience of trying to see clearly and objectively, the facilitator might bring up some particular challenges, such as the difficulty of evaluating students' questions. Ask the members, "What about student questions? Just out of curiosity, how many student questions did you find yourself recording?"

This topic—the student voice—can raise multiple observational difficulties. Generally, even when students appear relaxed about speaking up in class, it doesn't always mean they are comfortable discussing content. From my own rounds experience (and from research studies), I know that students rarely ask questions in school unless the questions are about procedural matters. Rounds participants need to be fully aware of what they are seeing and hearing in every portion of the instructional core.

The participants may also want to reflect on the connections between what they have learned in preparation for rounds and what they observe. Typical reflections include the following:

- "By looking at teaching and learning through what students make, do, say, or write, I learned about the connection, or lack of connection, between learning intentions and student tasks."
- "Watching the lesson progress, I could see cognitive demand deteriorating before my eyes."
- "From what I saw, the highest cognitive demand was in a kindergarten class."
- "Students worked hard without a single complaint despite work that was mainly recall."
- "I found it hard to observe without being evaluative or judgmental."

THE REAL WORK: FROM OBSERVATION NOTES TO EVIDENCE ON STICKY NOTES

After this warm-up discussion, the next phase of the agenda should be on beginning the real work: creating an evidence base by transferring selected observations onto sticky notes. This means having the participants translate their observation notes into useful pieces of evidence by writing down one piece of evidence onto one sticky note. This is a solitary activity. Many members create a pile in front of them of as many as five to ten notes per class, but there is no limit. Progressing through this part of the agenda may take as much as forty-five minutes during the first rounds session. The following section describes the process in detail.

Putting Relevant Evidence on Sticky Notes

Participants should transfer observation notes to sticky notes by going through their pages of notes and identifying items that are relevant to the problem of practice. Any material useful to analyzing the problem of practice should be copied onto sticky notes. The facilitator should tell the participants to keep track of which classroom generated which piece of evidence by writing on a corner of the sticky note a number representing each individual classroom. When, in the next stage, these notes are organized into patterns of practice, the network must know whether the evidence came from only one classroom or from a representative sample across a majority of classrooms. Being able to quickly link notes and particular classrooms is important when questions are raised.

Beginning with Generous Interpretations

Participants often struggle with which evidence is relevant to the problem of practice. You can urge members to incorporate a broad range of evidence at the start. Capturing a comprehensive sample of evidence helps draw a more objective, specific, and complete picture. It is particularly helpful in the first few rounds not to discard very much in this initial stage. Not all evidence warrants inclusion, yet at this point, it is difficult to determine which evidence is connected to the problem of practice. And while the group will eventually be discarding specific bits of evidence, this is generally better done during the next step, when the members analyze all the evidence together to discern patterns of teaching and learning. It is not until cause and effect are tested and sorted out that seemingly isolated or disconnected evidence either fits the rest of the picture or proves irrelevant.

Helpful Guidelines for Sticky-Note Procedures

Especially with participants in the first rounds sessions, it is helpful if the facilitators remind participants of the following guidelines for evaluating evidence.

Use One Sticky Note per Item of Evidence

Evidence should usually fit onto one sticky note. If it runs longer, this is generally an indication the note includes more than one item of evidence. You may want to help these writers sort out their observation into the discrete actions that took place.

Understand That Quotes Work Well

Quotes are great—they're specific and nonjudgmental and should always be framed by quotation marks. But if the evidence base only includes quotes, the richness of context, such as interactions within the instructional core, nonverbal events, and visual description, can be lost. Facilitators should point this out. Observers may confess they limited their notes to quotes because it felt safer. They should be encouraged instead, however, to capture a broader picture on future rounds visits.

Say What Did Occur, Not What Didn't

Network members should try their best to paint a picture of what actually does take place. The work of rounds is descriptive, but sometimes network members describe what they didn't see. This habit can be quite common. The authors of *Instructional Rounds* call it "the dog that didn't bark." Here are some examples: "The teacher didn't circulate around the room," or "The teacher didn't wait for the student to answer." Writing what one doesn't see implies judgment. In these instances, it is the facilitator's job to ask, "What did happen?" pressing participants to write what they *did* see or hear. There are usually ways of describing the same circumstances by restating the observation to something like "The teacher remained seated as students worked," or "The teacher asked a question and moved on." This might be the time to remind network members that it is up to the host schools, not the network, to decide what to do with such observations: to decide whether the picture provided is in need of change, and if so, whether to implement the network's recommendations.

Refer Questions Back to the Group

As facilitators circulate, members may have questions about whether a piece of evidence is sufficiently specific or nonjudgmental. Such questions are best referred back to their table group when it is time to screen the evidence.

Decide on How to Handle Facilitator Notes

Facilitators will have to decide what to do with their own notes, which may vary, depending on the group. If a facilitator decides to share them, it can be helpful to put them on display. People struggling with their own notes will find a facilitator's less-than-perfect notes encouraging. A facilitator may decide to give his or her notes to the observation team that the facilitator joined for observation in the classrooms. This may help fill out the team's observations, but the facilitator is unlikely to be joining the team to process the evidence during the debriefing process, as he or she will be leading the session.

Network members will become more adept at assessing evidence as they begin to grasp how teacher and student roles govern predictable interactions throughout all aspects of the instructional core.

THE TEAM SCREENING PROTOCOL, STAGE ONE

Once all the members of a team have transferred the items of evidence from their classroom observation notes onto sticky notes, it is time to screen the evidence. For this, the members work with their original classroom observation team to develop a comprehensive team evidence base. This process will take thirty to forty minutes.

The process for screening the evidence follows a careful protocol that was developed after my Australian colleague Karen Cain and I noticed that too lax a method led to poor evidence screening and a weak evidence base. Without a screening structure, the members began individually reviewing their colleagues' posts as they were written and posted, and not all posts were read when many were posted at the same time. Such informality meant a number of things began to happen: multiple side discussions would begin over different postings; a post would lead to several skeptical questions, which if embarrassing to the author, would cause the group to lapse into polite silence; individuals would become persistent advocates for their own notes; and different members would take responsibility for screening different sections of evidence, so that some members became familiar with only one section. In short, it wasn't always certain whether all evidence was receiving equal scrutiny and consideration during analysis.

The collegial reviewing of notes is integral to the rounds process, and this lack of organization compromised the network's ability to conduct a thorough evidence check with all members familiar with all evidence. A complete picture of a rounds visit does not develop until everyone is able to review all the evidence. Each post must be considered. Some might be replaced, removed, or slated for needing more attention, but all posts must be considered by the entire group. With these thoughts in mind, Cain and I developed what we called the *team screening protocol* for a more thorough, structured approach that helps generate a clean base of evidence.

As described in chapter 4, the facilitator begins by asking the observation team members to read each of their sticky notes aloud for review by their small group. Once the piece of evidence is determined to be specific and objective, it is placed at random on a large sheet of poster paper. Random placement is important because it means keeping an open mind about how the data will eventually be organized and arranged for further analysis. This cannot happen until the full body of evidence has been assembled and considered.

Things to Keep in Mind

In reviewing evidence, it is essential from the outset to hold the group to the strictly understood norms for quality data. This discussion will help members develop descriptive skills while encouraging them to focus on refining the evidence that has been gathered. No item of evidence can be posted until the small group has confirmed it as specific and objective. If any note raises questions, it can be revised, replaced, or removed. Here are some points to keep in mind as the group reviews the notes.

Even Apparently Identical Notes Are Valuable

Sometimes during screening, a participant declines to read a note, claiming it is identical to one already read. Every piece of evidence, however, should be reviewed, so that every member receives feedback from colleagues on the quality of his or her posts. A single word change or phrase can change meaning.

Multiple Perspectives Are Good

Multiple views of the same events are valued. Even though members may visit the same classrooms together, they are unlikely to see the same things. Different members talk privately with different students, may observe student work not seen by teammates, or may be the only one to catch particular details of a particular lesson. When the time comes to share these observations, many people are often surprised by what others may have noticed. The entire small group needs to hear every post.

Debate Is Healthy

Disagreements between members can be frequent. This is good. You want objective rigor and concrete evidence grounding the work unrestrained by the culture of nice. Interestingly, when disagreements are broken apart, it becomes apparent that they are often a reflection of incomplete evidence or members' having only a partial view of the moment being discussed. This is when I like to hear group members ask for more information or use the refrain "What's the evidence?" Discussions should begin and end with a concrete descriptive.

Juried Reviews Make for Stronger Evidence

Another benefit to these team discussions is that uncertainty is often resolved by the multiple viewpoints of juried reviews. Team approval is required for every post read aloud. In the end, the network benefits from the ultimate production of a quality body of evidence, team ownership of all evidence, and a well-informed team.

Common Problems, Suggested Solutions

Screening evidence is difficult the first time for most participants. Nonetheless, armed with knowledge about watching for evidence that is too general, too judgmental, or too full of jargon, the participants will find that it gets easier. See exhibit 6.1 for examples of evidence that didn't make the cut, and why. A number of problems commonly come up during this work. Let's look at some of these.

Teams Work Too Slowly

What can a facilitator do when some teams take a long time to finish their evidence posts, say, with one team only half finished while another is ready to begin the screening process? The work moves in a more timely fashion with smaller teams—no bigger than three or four. Each team should designate a table facilitator

---

EXHIBIT 6.1

Examples of Problematic Observations, with an Explanation of the Problem

- Class was fast paced. *(Judgmental)*
- Teacher asked questions about passages students just read. *(Too general)*
- Students practicing higher-order thinking skills. *(Too general and unclear)*
- Excellent classroom management. *(General and judgmental)*
- Teachers had students apply concept of fractions. *(Not enough information)*
- Too much time on discussion; not enough on individual work. *(Judgmental)*
- She did a great job transitioning class from group to independent work. *(Judgmental and uses jargon—who knows what "transitioning" means)*
- Teacher encourages students to think for themselves. *(Open to wide interpretation)*
- Teacher used interactive teaching style. *(Uses ill-defined jargon, too general)*
- The class was teacher directed. *(General, ill-defined)*

to oversee the timely completion of assignments. To help manage the process, the facilitator should regularly ask the table facilitators how much time their group needs to complete the task. By doing so, the groups also become more keenly aware of their own progress dynamic in relationship to other groups and work hard to catch up if necessary.

Teams Struggle with Their Screening Decisions

What about when members sometimes have trouble deciding whether a piece of evidence qualifies as specific enough or sufficiently objective and nonjudgmental? First off, congratulate them for challenging the evidence and then smile; agree they have a tough question, and ask them to let you know what they decide. But if they're still stuck on your next time around, you might suggest they look at the context of the event to be sure they are on the bottom of the ladder of inference. Other times, the issue can be too much information on one sticky note. It can help to ask the originator to explain, step by step, what took place in the classroom. Each step may warrant a post. Resolution may be found in a review of the small, discrete actions that everyone agrees on. The group can then ask the originator to rewrite the evidence to reflect what has been said aloud.

Teams Make Poor Screening Choices

What happens when evidence lacks clarity, is overly general, or is judgmental yet nonetheless has been accepted by the team? It is important from the beginning to establish a high standard for quality evidence. A facilitator should not hesitate to raise questions. If a sticky note reads, "The students worked in groups," ask for more information, such as whether that meant the students sat in groups or worked cooperatively as a group. You could also ask if the statement "worked in groups" in and of itself sheds useful light on the problem of practice. Frequently, more information is needed if the team is to understand the usefulness of such a post. If a note reads, "The students worked independently," ask if this meant they worked individually or they took responsibility for their work. When I am asked to parse a sticky note's meaning, I sometimes ask the originator to supply more information, because I have no way of knowing since I wasn't in the classroom with them.

Teams Begin Organizing Their Evidence

What if team members begin organizing the evidence on the poster paper as each piece is being screened? This happens a lot, and facilitators must watch for it. Even though protocol clearly calls for the screened evidence to be placed on poster paper at random, many find it difficult to resist organizing the material. They tend to want to make the process more manageable, but must refrain until they have all the evidence. Remind the teams that even when they have screened all their evidence, it represents only half of what will eventually be considered, since they will be pooling their evidence with another small team that also visited the same classrooms. It is premature, and not fair to the host school or to the other team, to develop groupings of any sort before all the evidence is considered.

THE TEAM SCREENING PROTOCOL, STAGE TWO

In the second stage of the screening protocol, the two teams that observed the same classrooms will pool their data to form a comprehensive picture of the visited classrooms. The first step is to have each small team review its partner team's evidence before the two teams are joined. When the small teams vet their partner team's evidence, both teams become thoroughly familiar with the other half of the evidence that will be pooled for the comprehensive picture.

Problems with Pooling the Evidence

Early in my work as a rounds facilitator, I used to have each small team create patterns directly from the evidence they screened from the four classrooms they had visited. The teams took from forty-five minutes to an hour to discuss, debate, hone, and, finally, adopt their own patterns according to their ideas on how to organize the material. Once finished, the pairs of small teams were merged, each team with patterns in hand. This merger resulted in one new, midsized team tasked to combine the separate patterns into one body of organized data.

Armed with the patterns they had just developed, the teams would begin presenting their work. This process took another hour. The problem was that these midsized teams had a hard time agreeing on how to merge their two separate findings into one coherent analysis. After having spent an hour invested in one plan, many team members found it stressful to then have to find a way to agree on something new. Neither small team was completely familiar with the evidence base of its partner team, because each team spent more time defending its own individual patterns than looking at the other team's evidence. Much time was spent in argument over how to merge evidence, half of which the teams knew well (their own), with too much of the other half unknown (their partner team's). Throughout this process, each team would promote, explain, and justify the patterns it had spent so much time developing.

Pooling evidence can create a very different picture from what each small team might base its initial patterns on, even though both had visited the same four classrooms, so the members often felt they had wasted their time. I recall one midsized team so angry and unable to come to any agreement on a set of patterns, it declared a stalemate.

The Red-Dot Protocol

The red-dot protocol, described below and in exhibit 6.2, helps the two small teams join to form a midsized team through the way evidence is screened and organized. With this approach, no patterns are created until all members of the soon-to-be paired teams have separately rescreened each other's evidence before pooling both

---

EXHIBIT 6.2

Steps for the Red-Dot Protocol

1. Small teams exchange poster papers of evidence yielded from the team screening protocol of their partner team (the small team that saw the same classrooms at different times) and return to their own table with the other team's evidence in hand.

2. Each small team screens the evidence of their partner team, following the same procedure specified in the team screening protocol by reading aloud one piece of evidence at a time for screening.

3. As each team screens the evidence, it places a red sticky dot on pieces of evidence that are judgmental, too general, or simply unclear. Evidence that raises questions—even material that appears objective and specific—should be red-dotted so that everyone has clarity about all the evidence.

4. Once both teams have screened all the evidence, the two pull their tables together to resolve the notes that have red dots. As before, evidence that does not pass reinspection may be rewritten, corrected, or tossed. Completion of this step means that the body of evidence from both teams has become pooled as one evidence base owned by all, and this new, midsized team is now ready to begin pattern development.

---

sets. This protocol takes about twenty minutes and leaves both teams completely familiar with the entire database before they initiate patterns. It also creates a much safer place for the members to forcefully question evidence without personal confrontation. Facilitators should remind the group to value the integrity of the work, which importantly means overcoming a culture of nice.

A larger amount of evidence is more complicated to analyze, but the resulting patterns represent a more comprehensive picture of what went on in the classroom and, by extension, school-wide. This yields the high-quality data needed for analysis.

Exchanging Evidence for Screening

The red dot protocol begins with the exchange of evidence. First, each team in the room hands over its poster paper of random sticky notes to its soon-to-be paired classroom-visit partner. Second, all the teams then separately review their partner team's evidence. To review their partner's sticky notes, the team members read each note aloud one at a time to their small team. They then mark each piece of evidence they consider unclear, too general, or judgmental, with a small sticky red dot. Evidence that raises questions—even material that appears objective and specific—should also be red-dotted so that it is flagged for discussion. The anonymity of checking evidence written by others not present at the table helps yield a more objective picture of classroom action. If you see teams hesitant to use red dots, remind them that it is better to clarify their doubts now than to assume that all is fine and let a questionable piece of evidence slide by. To encourage them to use the dots, you might also inform them that their partner team isn't hesitating to do so, if that is the case.

Rescreening in Midsized Teams

Once all the evidence is screened, the small teams then pull their tables together to form a midsized team. (They will remain a midsized team until the end of this rounds visit.) Their job now is to resolve questions about the red-dot items. They begin by appointing a facilitator for the midsized team—someone who will keep an eye on the time, keep the group on track, and encourage all to participate—and a scribe, who will become active in the next phase when it comes time to write the patterns down on poster paper.

During this final review, red dots can only be removed when questions are fully resolved and understood by all. As before, the evidence in question may be revised, rewritten, or removed until the entire midsized team is satisfied. When an item is questioned, it is not unusual for someone from the team that had done the initial screening to say, "Yes, I agree. We tried to tell John, but he said we were too picky," or "We discussed that but couldn't decide." This means that the team originally screening the evidence had not thoroughly resolved the issue.

Strong, Honed Data

At the end of the red-dot protocol, the team should be confident that what is left is honed data—a useful body of evidence for the analysis of teaching and learning practice in the host school. Facilitators should remind team members at this time that once items pass the team screening, the entire team owns the results. (Sometimes members keep informal personal tallies of how many of their sticky notes receive red dots from session to session, and then tally how many red dots their team incurs from one session to the next. They generally notice that over time, fewer and fewer red dots appear, attesting to their increased skill.)

Challenges to the Red-Dot Protocol

Facilitators should be prepared to reassure anxious members that though the work is challenging, it will get easier as their skills improve. You may hear doubts and frustrations, with participants wondering things like "Will I be able to do this?" or "Will I ever get better?" The ability to yield high-quality evidence from classroom observations requires "practice, practice, practice," to quote City and the coauthors of *Instructional Rounds*. Sometimes it helps to invite the members to reflect from time to time on how far they have come in their practice. Facilitators can learn a lot about the way members go about classroom observations by monitoring their use of the red-dot protocol.

I recall a case where a team had nearly finished screening yet had not attached a single red dot. A screened-evidence sheet without red dots is extraordinarily unusual in the first few rounds and caught my attention. When I asked about it, one member said in frustration that the posts all contained simple quotes, nothing else. Sometimes this kind of thing escapes the facilitator's notice, no matter how watchful he or she is during the earlier screening process. In these cases, the issue belongs to the team that generated the evidence, not the team using the dots. I use the moment to explain that quote-only notes present limited potential for comprehensive analysis. I also assure the "quote-only team" that a comprehensive analysis is still possible if their partner team collected additional evidence beyond quotes.

As the morning session ends and before the group breaks for lunch, facilitators should ask the members to reflect on their personal growth and that of the network in the morning rounds activities, from classroom observation to sticky notes to the screening and organization of evidence.

LAST THOUGHTS

Notes Are Private; Sticky Notes Are Eventually Destroyed

Facilitators should have already made it clear to members that observation notes remain in the private hands of the writer and that sticky notes never leave the room. This practice encourages members to take notes without worrying about offending individual teachers. It also means the members can be very candid. The concern with the sticky notes is that these stark observations can be linked to a specific classroom. Although frank, unrestricted discussion is necessary for analysis, it is also why these notes must be kept private and why sticky notes are destroyed. The results of rounds visits that are shared with the host schools are released as statements describing patterns of practice or as descriptive summaries of what was seen in a majority of the school's classrooms—not observations about individual classrooms or teachers.

Screening Evidence: The Takeaway

The most important task for facilitators during this part of the rounds process is to keep a close eye on the quality of evidence being generated, because it represents the integrity of the work. Facilitators must encourage the network members to overcome the culture of nice. These two aspects of rounds—quality and candor—always need monitoring. Even experienced networks can sometimes become too casual in their development of an evidence base. They might be tempted to take shortcuts, jump too quickly to conclusions, fail to give forthright evaluations, or skip important steps of the process. When this happens, opportunities for deeper learning are lost. By following the recommendations in this chapter, network members can refine their evidence-only gathering skills and become good, hard-nosed screeners of data.

CHAPTER 7

Developing Patterns and Making Predictions

A fter a busy morning observing in classrooms and refining the evidence, the network members break for lunch (which is often catered sandwiches in the meeting space). As they enjoy this well-earned downtime, the facilitator should ask that if they discuss the work, they remain in the descriptive voice.

After lunch, the next phase will be about making sense of the honed evidence. The members do this while the evidence is laid out before them. This will take their hard work to the next level and will take most of the afternoon.

The network members will be organizing the evidence to discover patterns of classroom interactions between teacher, student, and curriculum content—patterns that reveal important clues about student learning and the school's problem of practice. With these patterns established, the network will then make predictions about student learning. When taken all together, these patterns and predictions should suggest areas of focus for school improvement.

For this work, the network will be moving up the ladder of inference from gathering and screening observations for objective substance, to organizing this evidence for meaning. Although this involves moving from nonjudgmental observing to summarizing and analyzing, it still must be accomplished with deliberate rigor. Again, the network members will need to beware of framing their work on a foundation of false assumptions. Fortunately, the rigor of the rounds process again offers help in the form of structured protocols to guide network members every step of the way.

This chapter begins by delineating the process of making patterns. Next, it explains how these patterns are used to predict what the students can be expected to learn as a result of their education in this school and how these same predictions can then lead to recommendations for school improvement.

IDENTIFYING PATTERNS

The patterns that network members glean from looking over vetted evidence reveal much about the interactions within the instructional core that can support or hinder progress on the problem of practice. In organizing the evidence, the network's goal is to identify patterns useful to school improvement efforts by generating comprehensive descriptions that enable deeper understanding of the problem with student learning. As distillations of current practice, patterns reveal the hard edges of what is taking place in teaching and learning in the classroom. The ability to clearly see current classroom practice leads to understanding what needs to change to improve student outcomes.

The key to describing patterns is to let the evidence paint a picture of what takes place. Specific and nonjudgmental evidence is what gives the work integrity, and making sense of this evidence—clean observations about the instructional core—is the work of patterns.

Returning to Midsized Teams

Begin by asking the network members to return to their midsized-team tables. Each team of six to eight is composed of the two small teams that separately visited the same classrooms. This means that everyone on the team has vetted and is familiar with the same evidence base. (Depending on the size of the network—I usually have four or five midsized teams—this may represent a sample of sixteen to twenty classrooms visited across the school.)

As they settle in, remind them of some of the sample patterns discussed during the launch session to refresh their memory of what they're looking for—in form, content, and syntax. A month or more may have passed since the launch session, and reminders of these earlier lessons can be helpful.

Determining the Form, Content, and Syntax of Patterns

Remind members that in terms of *form*, they're looking for sentences that are simple, declarative statements summarizing patterns of evidence from what they observed. The *content* of these statements should relate something about the instructional core and how it is connected in some way to the school's problem of practice. And for *syntax*, they should understand that meaning can change significantly, depending on what words are used and how they are phrased.

In essence, then, these statements need to be about a pattern that has been seen and has bearing on what the school needs to know to improve learning in their classrooms. Moreover, the statements need to be stated in such a way as to be accurate and exacting yet able to be heard by their intended audience.

Grouping Sticky Notes

The teams now get to work grouping their sticky notes. Teams find wall space or tables to display, study, and discuss their sheets of evidence. Some teams may begin by moving their sticky notes into categories such as teacher or student questions, group work, teacher actions, student comments, or perhaps the three elements of the instructional core. Other teams may start by talking about which of their observations across the four classrooms have relevance to the problem of practice. Each team develops its own way of working, but eventually the members move the evidence (sticky notes) into groups that make sense to them.

As the teams form patterns, they search for commonalities—patterns must contain evidence from a majority of classrooms observed—and titles that serve as an overarching descriptive sentence that embodies the import of the related sticky notes. Each group of sticky notes is stuck on the poster paper under the corresponding descriptive sentence. This way, once the patterns are completed, they can be displayed for presentation for network review with the appended supporting evidence if justification is needed.

Making Judgments and Drawing Conclusions

By their nature, patterns climb the ladder of inference because judgment is used to organize evidence in a way that makes sense. Patterns nonetheless must be written in evidence-only language, and the statement that summarizes each trait must reflect something common, as noted above, to all the sticky notes in the group. See exhibit 7.1 for examples of the strong, clear statements you're looking for.

Pattern statements are productive when they communicate the intended message clearly and accurately and are supported by the evidence written on sticky notes arrayed around the statements. Their wording should be thoughtfully expressed to increase receptivity from the host school, but should not compromise on meaning, regardless of the impact on host school staff and faculty.

It will take the midsized teams from ninety minutes to two hours to develop patterns from their evidence. The new screening protocols will help them along, especially since all the members of the midsized teams are familiar with all the evidence and the members don't begin to develop patterns until the two small teams have united as one midsized group. (Nonetheless, this work always takes

---

EXHIBIT 7.1

Sample Pattern Statements

- Teachers moved on after one correct response.
- Students asked five questions, all procedural.
- A select group of students answered teacher's questions.
- Teachers asked students to solve problems in their own way.
- Students worked cooperatively in groups to solve problems.
- Twenty-four of twenty-eight students said they would know they'd done well when the teacher said so.

---

longer with district-wide teams who fear offending their colleagues. They perseverate, often triple-checking their work to make sure the evidence substantiates the patterns, and agonize over the wording of their statements.)

COMMON DIFFICULTIES IN MAKING PATTERNS

As discussed, teasing out the patterns from a mass of evidence requires thoughtful, open discussion and thorough analysis. To make sure that the teams' efforts represent time well spent, facilitators should be on the lookout for unhelpful habits that drain this exercise of its usefulness.

Creating Patterns in Search of Evidence

As facilitator, you need to make sure that the patterns are derived from evidence rather than what I call "creating a pattern in search of evidence." In the latter case, the members come up with a pattern based upon their overall impressions of evidence and then hunt for sticky notes to prove that the pattern exists. Facilitators should wonder what is happening when a pattern is written on poster paper before sticky notes are grouped. When I ask, I often hear something like, "We think this pattern statement is true, but are looking to make sure there is evidence to support it." In cases like this, tell the members that it is better to begin by moving sticky notes into groups before writing a pattern and let the description of each group determine how you define the patterns. In a sense, it is the similarity of evidence in a group that writes the pattern.

This work is cognitively demanding, and facilitators must not do the work for the teams. The facilitators' questions at this time serve to model the kind of grilling each team should expect when they present their completed patterns for network vetting. For this reason, most teams are eager to run their patterns by the facilitator for early feedback.

Focusing Too Much on the Teacher

Members new to the rounds process often return from classroom visits with numerous observations about what the teacher was up to, while having few notes about students or content. The observers often don't realize this until they begin to group their notes into patterns. Such one-sided observations are obviously a relic of teacher-focused approaches to understanding student learning. In these situations, facilitators should discuss what observation strategies led to these teacher-focused notes and suggest that members consider and make journal notes about how to improve their methods next time for gathering evidence related to problems of practice.

Failing to Record Something Important, but Remembering It Later

While creating patterns, the participants sometimes realize they saw something of importance, but failed to record it in their observation notes. Tell them it is never too late to create a sticky from observation notes, but if the event, however, never made it into their observation notes in the first place, then including the event is a bit riskier, but still workable. As long as the individual is absolutely certain the reporting is accurate, a sticky note may be written. The point is not to limit information, but to make sure every bit of evidence is accurate, specific, and true to the event.

A Sticky Note That Can Serve More Than One Pattern

The participants may worry about and debate placing one piece of evidence in a group when perhaps it is better placed in another group. This is actually not a problem. Tell the participants they can simply duplicate the sticky note and use it in more than one group.

Too Much Content

Sometimes teams group a large amount of evidence together and then get tangled in a debate over the wording of the pattern. They may find that more than one sentence describes parts but not the entirety of the evidence. They then try to solve this problem by adding more words or joining partly descriptive sentences to form the pattern. This is usually a red flag that more than one pattern has been grouped together. In these cases, you might suggest that the team members ask themselves whether there are a couple of smaller patterns hidden in the larger group of evidence.

Loosely Defined Language

If teams are stuck, try asking them to read aloud what they have written. More often than not, you hear words that are too general or unclear. One example of this might be "Lessons were teacher-centered." In this case, facilitators should ask what *teacher-centered* means. Or you might ask, "What told you the lessons were teacher-centered? What took place that caused you to use the term *teacher-centered*?" These questions require a team to break down the meaning of the term. When asked, the members will often give responses like "The teachers asked all the questions," "The teachers did all the talking," "The teachers gave praise," "All the discussions went from the teacher to the student and back to the teacher," or other descriptions of classroom dynamics that might fit into the catchall term *teacher-centered*.

Each of the above responses could form a separate pattern. Patterns are more productive when narrowed to concrete descriptions that help the host school staff understand the meaning of a specific activity within their classrooms. Such descriptions target particular behaviors that work to undermine or promote better student learning.

Facilitators can help teams develop more productive patterns by asking, "If you were a teacher in this school and received a pattern that said the lessons were teacher-centered, would you know exactly what was taking place, and what you would need to do differently if you wanted to change that?" Questions like these help the members reflect on the potential interpretations of their description of a pattern. You might suggest that teams use each other as sounding boards, one team asking another to tell them behaviors they think the pattern is describing. Testing specificity with another team is often what authors do to determine whether their writing is clear.

Misunderstanding Teacher Praise

Teacher feedback is rarely the direct topic of patterns, yet you'll see a lot of pattern statements like "Teachers encouraged students in their work," or "Teachers gave recognition to good work." When asked what evidence gave rise to the pattern, members usually respond that teachers said things like "Good job," "Right," and "Very good" in all the classes. The facilitator should press the team to be more specific about describing the teacher comments, all of which express a teacher's favorable evaluation of student work. As such, they do form a pattern of feedback, but it is of a particular kind: praise. Unfortunately, praise by the teacher turns out to be the least productive kind of feedback—if not counterproductive feedback—because it creates teacher dependency. But because praise is such a significant component of teacher practice, facilitators should note that productive uses of the various types of feedback warrant further discussion. This is a good topic for further network study because when used expertly, feedback is a powerful tool to promote student learning, more powerful than the skillful asking of questions.

Misinterpreting the Teacher's Checking for Understanding

A related common observation about teacher behavior is what can be called *checking for understanding*. When members write, "The teachers checked for understanding," the facilitator should ask what they mean by this pattern statement. The most frequent reply is that they knew that the teachers were checking for understanding because the teachers had asked the students if they understood.

Facilitators should always follow this up with a question like, "And did the students understand?" or "Does the evidence show that the teachers now know who understands and who doesn't?" or "Was it apparent that the teachers found out whether students understood?" Often, the members reply they don't know or that the teachers asked a question but moved on without receiving a response.

Facilitators should remind the members that if they can't see it, it isn't there. The team can observe what the teachers did: they asked whether students understood. But the team cannot observe why the teachers asked the question. In this case, the members have ascribed a motive to teachers' actions without evidence that student understanding was ever checked. If the sticky notes state that the teachers did not receive a response, did not act upon responses given by the students, or accepted one correct answer and moved on, then these actions should also be reflected in patterns, in addition to the statement "Teachers asked if students understood." Otherwise, a pattern worded as "Teachers checked for understanding" presents a picture that would be misleading to the network and host staff.

School Programs in Transition

A school in transition is something facilitators should be aware of. Networks sometimes visit schools that are in the middle of implementing new teaching methods or new programs—say, *math talk*, an improvement strategy to develop student mathematical thinking.

If, for example, a math-talk program at a school has as yet only reached half the math classes school-wide, observations across the school would probably then reflect these different approaches and therefore appear skewed or uneven. In these cases, conflicting patterns may result, depending on which classes were visited. When patterns contrast from one team to another, it is often a sign that a school is in an improvement transition. It is helpful to represent both patterns, not only because they portray what was seen by each team (assuming the patterns were properly substantiated), but also because they tell a more complete story about the host school.

Teams Finishing at Different Times

A large time block is reserved for pattern development, and inevitably a couple of teams will finish before others. Sometimes an early finish is an indication that a team has missed some complexity. It is important that the teams do a thorough job. You can check the teams' work to determine if their patterns could benefit from greater clarity or whether the patterns sufficiently explored the problem of practice. I sometimes reference the principal's opening presentation about the kind of evidence the host school was especially interested in, to see if there is anything more they wish to contribute.

But if the teams' work looks solid, and it looks as if the slower teams will be finished before long, early finishers can set up their pattern displays and take a short break. Doing so prepares them for the next step and tips off the slower teams that time is running out.

Another option that facilitators can turn to in these cases is to challenge the early-finishing teams with an exercise designed to encourage them to think about cognitive demand in the classroom. In particular, facilitators can ask the teams to explore what happens to the level of cognitive demand between the times a teacher gives an assignment and when the students complete the related tasks. This analysis may not be directly tied to the host school's particular problem of practice, but it often is, and if not, it still advances deeper network learning. (If cognitive demand is indeed related to the school's problem of practice, you could ask the entire network to do this exercise, as time allows.) If the members don't have specific notes related to cognitive demand, they can still do the exercise by reviewing their observation notes on the assignments and the work the students were doing.

First, ask them to recall each assignment created by the teacher and to categorize it as either of low or of high cognitive demand. The participants record this observation by making a mark on the chart in the appropriate quadrant. Second, have the participants categorize the tasks or work that the students actually did to complete the assignment, and have them enter the data onto a chart as they did for the teacher's assignments (see exhibit 7.2 for results compiled from multiple teaching episodes observed by one large network on one rounds visit). The completed chart illustrates what often happens to the level of cognitive demand from when a teacher gives the assignment to when the students do the work. In conducting this exercise, the group may find that many assignments start out at a higher demand (such as conceptual work that requires students to justifying their thinking, and work requiring more than recall and understanding) than may be found in the work the students eventually do. Such was the case for the network example shown in exhibit 7.2. Cognitive demand deteriorates as the lesson unfolds—an unintended decline that shows up in what students make, do, say, or write.

A study by educators James Hiebert and James Stigler ("A World of Difference: Classrooms Abroad Provide Lessons in Teaching Math and Science," in *Secondary Lenses on Learning Participant Book: Team Leadership for Mathematics in Middle and High Schools*, ed. Catherine Miles Grant, Valerie L. Mills, Mary Bouck, and Ellen Davidson [Thousand Oaks, CA: Corwin, 2009], 77) shows that when working on conceptual problems, teachers in the United States "rarely provided students an opportunity to explore and discuss mathematical relationships . . . They almost always stepped in and did the work for the student or ignored the conceptual aspect of the problem when discussing it." The authors assert this deterioration of cognitive demand in the classroom is substantially responsible for the underperformance of American students on international tests.

PRESENTING AND VETTING PATTERNS

As soon as the teams complete organizing their sticky notes into patterns and create overarching statements that reflect the content of these patterns, ask them to

EXHIBIT 7.2		
Debriefing Cognitive Demand		
	Cognitive Demand	
	Low	**High**
Assignment (what the teacher assigns)	13	16
Task (the work the students do)	26	4

put their poster papers up for display, again reminding slower teams that time is nearly up. Once all the posters are completed, the teams will present their pattern statements and their accompanying evidence to the entire network for vetting.

Presenting Patterns to the Network

The facilitator should ask the teams to label their set of patterns (perhaps three to seven from each group) with their team designation before presenting them for network review. Each team begins by reading the pattern statements aloud consecutively without stopping so the network can get a sense of the scope of work, before the team presents them one by one for discussion. These pattern statements distill the essence of what the network has observed of teaching and learning in the host school's classrooms and will be the summary statements that the host school staff receives.

The Vetting Process

As each team reads its patterns aloud, one pattern at a time, the network's job is to assess whether the descriptive statement is clear and the evidence supports, explains, and matches the statement. In this way, accuracy is honed and phrasing is clarified. As each pattern is read, the facilitator should ask if further clarification is needed. If no comments come forth, the facilitator should just wait and then press further by asking if the silence means everyone agrees with the statement's wording and connection to the problem of practice. It is of strategic importance that members understand that the accepted patterns represent the integrity of their work. Each statement needs to be discussed as if each were being challenged—which is something that very well may happen when the statements are shown to the faculty at the host school. So it is critical that all the statements can be substantiated and are clear. This is the network's last chance to consider them before signing off, which is when the statements become work they own. This final discussion may take some time; it must be rigorous and thorough.

Challenging the Pattern Statements

In challenging the pattern statements, the members should again ask, "What's the evidence?" Evidence notes are a team's only line of justification. If the evidence does not justify the pattern, the statement fails. Sometimes, when a team is asked to justify its assertion by reading aloud its evidence notes, the team members begin to pick and choose from among the sticky notes that back up their statement. This is an indication that something may be questionable about the evidence, in which case they should be asked to share all the evidence for that pattern for network evaluation.

In other instances, a member of the network may question an assertion: "Our team didn't see any teacher questions about recall and understanding, but this pattern says their team saw many." In cases like this, where different teams see different patterns, there are three possible explanations:

1. The pattern is not substantiated by the evidence and requires rethinking.
2. The pattern is substantiated, unlike the contrasting pattern created by the other team.
3. Both patterns are substantiated. The patterns show contrasting scenes because the midsized teams visited different groups of classrooms, or the school may be in transition, or both.

It is then up to the network to decide which of the above possibilities explains the differences between the teams' patterns.

After all the patterns are presented, each team takes time to revise its pattern statements, if necessary, while the facilitators circulate and intervene or assist as needed.

SUCCESSFUL SAMPLE PATTERNS EXPLAINED

Exhibit 7.3 presents some samples of pattern statements approved by networks. We will discuss them in pairs to illustrate contrasting features, why they were accepted, and what they communicate.

These statements were composed during various rounds visits by midsized teams that observed in the four classrooms they visited (at different times as two separate teams). Reminder: a pattern is not warranted unless it reflects the practice of a majority of the classrooms or the teaching or learning episodes observed.

Patterns A and B: *Students answered all teacher questions correctly* and *Students discussed the content of the lesson in small groups*. These pattern statements express what occurred in most circumstances observed. The wording indicates the extent of the occurrence—a general pattern with few exceptions. Facilitators should tell the network members that when these patterns are presented to the host school, the in-network host school staff will be able to field questions and clearly explain the meaning of the patterns.

Patterns C and D: *In six of eight classrooms, teachers called on students with hands raised* and *In three of four classrooms, a select group of students answered all the questions*. These patterns were seen in a majority of classrooms, but are qualified by the actual number of classrooms. This phrasing occurs because members feel

---

EXHIBIT 7.3

Successfully Vetted Pattern Statements

A. Students answered all teacher questions correctly.

B. Students discussed the content of the lesson in small groups.

C. In six of eight classrooms, teachers called on students with hands raised.

D. In three of four classrooms, a select group of students answered all the questions.

E. When forty-three students were asked, "Is this work easy or challenging?" twenty-nine said it was easy.

F. Of twenty-eight teacher questions recorded, twenty-six were at a recall or understanding level.

G. Tasks were inconsistent with the stated focus of the lesson.

H. Assignments matched or exceeded grade-level content standards.

---

uncomfortable making statements worded as strongly as the first two—in that while the statements reflect a majority of observations, there were exceptions. Notice that one statement refers to eight classrooms, while the other to four. Despite visiting the same four classrooms, this midsized team developed patterns based on the observation of eight separate teaching or learning sessions. As long as the pattern wording is justified by the evidence and is communicated clearly, it works. Again, the host school network members can explain this to faculty and staff.

Patterns E and F: *When forty-three students were asked, "Is this work easy or challenging?" twenty-nine said it was easy* and *Of twenty-eight teacher questions recorded, twenty-six were at a recall or understanding level.* These two pattern statements represent the results of asking students the same questions in multiple classrooms. (Notice that pattern F in particular reflects the use of Bloom's Revised Taxonomy to decide on the level of thinking required of students. The network will find it helpful to use this taxonomy or something similar in all sessions for member reference, and classifications like these may be a good topic for an in-service session.) Again, the numbers in these two statements inform staff of the extent of the evidence; raw numbers are preferred over percentages, because percentiles mean little to the school if only a small number of students were asked.

If team observers were only to ask the students an initial question, the evidence base would be nothing more than what a school might accomplish by giving a survey. But when network members dig deeper by asking follow-up questions, student responses have more meaning. Host schools may find some patterns hard to accept, and follow-up questions provide additional information that increases staff understanding and thoughtful consideration. Material gleaned from follow-up questions is helpful when included in patterns and reported to the school. For example, if a student claims that the work was easy, a follow-up question may reveal that the work was easy because the student did the same work last year or that all the answers were in the paragraph preceding the questions.

Patterns G and H: *Tasks were inconsistent with the stated focus of the lesson* and *Assignments matched or exceeded grade-level content standards.* Comments like these can only be made when the members are knowledgeable about the classroom curriculum. Members are generally hesitant to comment directly on teacher decisions about lesson and content.

Pattern G communicates a difference between what the teacher intends for the students to learn and what the students are actually doing. This is objective and specific and therefore helpful feedback.

Pattern H communicates the relationship of assignments to curriculum frameworks, which the members would need to be familiar with to make this observation. If the members were unfamiliar with the curriculum standards, then the standards might be a helpful resource document during rounds. (This may be something facilitators and think-tank members should discuss as a topic for a future in-service.)

A FINAL REVIEW OF PATTERNS BY NETWORK AND HOST SCHOOL MEMBERS

After the pattern statements have cleared the vetting process, this material, along with the network's predictions (discussed later in this chapter) will ultimately be given to the host school principal at the end of the rounds session on the second day. Since the host school network members are those with the greatest stakes in the outcome of the analysis, the facilitator should ask them how prepared they feel to present these pattern statements to their faculty colleagues. They will need to be absolutely confident they understand and can explain the content of each statement. Remind them that their job is to neither justify nor defend, but that they will need to answer questions to clarify what the faculty and staff don't understand.

They should also be prepared to detail how the rounds process produced these patterns. So as the group moves through the final review, be sure to ask the host school members whether they understand each statement completely or have questions about whether the pattern is substantiated by the evidence. Once these concerns are put to rest, the network signs off on the statements. The patterns are then ready to be printed out for the host school at the end of the last day.

When you are preparing documents for the host school and for network member records, and to enable easier communication within the network and across the district, it helps to have the pattern statements printed out in a clear and consistent format. These statements do not, of course, include the evidence-containing sticky notes.

Sticky Note Hygiene

As teams move to the final stages to generate predictions and develop the next level of work during this rounds visit, the members often find it helpful to refer back to the patterns and supporting documentation of sticky notes. Sticky notes are critical records that do not get destroyed until the members are ready to leave the rounds session.

Facilitators Establish a Record of Patterns Across a District

Facilitators should establish a file of the patterns developed in every rounds session to use to assess network and host school progress. Should a school hold a second or third rounds visit, a comparison of the new patterns to the first rounds patterns is instructive. Should a school district wish to develop a district-wide problem of practice, commonalities of patterns across schools over time can be determined from this resource. As networks grow in their command of the rounds process, it can be illuminating to consider two problems of practice: one generated by a host school and one discerned from patterns district-wide. Patterns are also a useful resource in offering baseline comparison points to measure the effectiveness of a theory of action to achieve long-term improvement. (More will be said about this in chapter 9.)

PREDICTIONS

The next phase in the rounds process takes place before the end of the first day and involves making predictions, a deceptively valuable link to understanding the cause and effect of teaching and learning. This step predicts what students would know and be able to do as a result of attending the host school, given how the patterns describe the interactions around the school's instructional core. In this phase of rounds, the network members should begin to think about what kind of students they are creating at their own schools as well.

What Are Predictions?

The authors of *Instructional Rounds* say that predictions address the question "If you were a student in this school and you did everything you were expected to do, what would you know and be able to do?" The phrase "you did everything you were expected to do" requires astute observation in the classroom. Teacher expectations are largely expressed through stated learning intentions and assignments, but expectations are altered when the teachers do the work for the students, simplify assignments during the course of instruction, or accept less rigorous work as satisfying the demands of the intended assignments.

When asked to make predictions, network members are often confused and wonder what predictions have to do with rounds. It seems disconnected from what they have been doing so far in trying for objectivity. It can seem too far up the ladder of inference. Many members ask whether making predictions means "what students think they are expected to do, and if so, should we ask them, and is this the same thing that teachers ask or want students to do?" The answer is that their predictions should address the question "What would students in this school know and be able to do in light of the patterns observed?"

What Patterns Tell Us About Predictions

Patterns reflect what students do in response to what is expected of them explicitly and implicitly. As we know from the principles of the instructional core, what students make, do, say, or write is the best predictor of performance and, therefore, the best predictor of what they should know and are able to do. This should be evident in the patterns. If the nature of student performance cannot be determined by the patterns, then there is inadequate evidence to make predictions.

Predictions Connect Analysis to Improvement

Predictions form the middle link between patterns and the next level of work, and it is not until this link is missing that we appreciate its role. When we begin with a problem of practice to guide classroom observation, we analyze the interactions within the instructional core in order to build a picture of the nature of the teaching and learning in relation to the problem of practice. From this picture of teaching and learning, we predict what the students should know and be able to do. If the predictions fall short of school goals, the questions become "What is the difference between these predictions and the desired school outcomes, and how do we fix it?" "How do we close the gap between what we predict students would know and be able to do and what we would like to enable them to do?" The next level of work, which is about how to close that gap, is based on a shared understanding of the learning we would like to see in juxtaposition to what we see. This gap drives purposeful action.

Sharing Predictions

Facilitators may wish to provide samples of predictions as a way to help members understand how to make their own. Members appreciate reading predictions made by teachers in prior host schools. This helps the members overcome their fear that their predictions will be too painful for the host school faculty and staff to entertain. See exhibit 7.4 for some sample predictions. Note that these predictions could describe the students' capabilities in their next school year or after graduation. The team can decide the time frame.

Predictions should not be directly shared with host school faculty other than those within the network, because predictions are conjecture despite being derived from evidence. Faculty can get stuck on predictions and become defensive when they are shared. Reactions like "How can they say that? They don't really understand what is going on here" are common. Instead, facilitators should suggest that the principals have faculty members make their own predictions, once the patterns from the network have been discussed.

EXHIBIT 7.4

Sample Predictions

- Students will walk away with little ability to demonstrate their own thinking without teacher direction.
- Students will leave the school comfortably locked into routines; they may struggle to think deeply and work as independent individuals.
- Students will take responsibility for and initiate their own learning.
- Students will know that if they hesitate, someone else will do the work.

Making Predictions

Each team develops predictions using its own patterns as a starting point. It may also use patterns created by the other teams if the patterns are consistent with its own findings. Teams are given about ten to fifteen minutes to prepare and write their predictions on poster paper to be shared with the network.

For each prediction, the network audience should ask what specific teaching and learning evidence supports the assertion. The similarities and differences between the predictions are worth consideration. Predictions from one team may contradict another team's, but as discussed earlier, the differences may arise because teams have observed different classrooms or because the school is in transition and is therefore likely to produce varying patterns and predictions. Finally, facilitators should ask what implications these predictions pose for the next level of work.

Difficulty in Making and Receiving Predictions

Some members will feel uncomfortable with making predictions and sit back while the remainder of the group moves ahead. The host school staff often finds predictions difficult to consider because they raise serious questions about student outcomes. Network members may also become somewhat timid when host members are sitting in the group, because the nonhost members do not want to offend.

It is helpful to address this before the predictions phase begins. Take the host school participants aside, and invite them to assume the role of listener-at-large, rather than participant, from this point forward. Host school participants find it challenging to participate objectively in predictions and may inhibit creative network responses in the next-level-of-work phase. The role of listener-at-large helps the highly vested members step back to see their school in a new light. Most feel caught between their loyalty to their hardworking colleagues and the new (and more objectively critical) view they are gaining of their school through their participation in rounds work. (If the network contains more than one person from the host school, you can suggest they consider forming their own group to make predictions and do the next level of work when that time comes.)

Wanting to Make Nice Predictions

The culture of nice may lead network members to use predictions as an opportunity to be sure that at least some good things are said, regardless of the evidence. When this happens, members need to be reminded that what is documented in patterns is neither good nor bad: it is one point in an improvement cycle. If the school has identified a problem of practice, the network should expect to see a problem. People do a disservice to the school and especially the students if they shrink from providing an accurate picture. Remind the members that they help the school when they work diligently to ensure strong cause-and-effect correlations between the evidence and the predictions they are making. From here, the network can begin to see where to initiate school improvement efforts.

Time Overruns

As the afternoon is drawing to a close, it is likely that many of the activities will have taken longer than anticipated. This almost always happens, especially with the first few schools' rounds visits. Unfortunately, it is hard to curtail any piece of the agenda. Predictions contribute to understanding and link to the next level of work. In a pinch, facilitators can give the teams five minutes to discuss predictions, and then can open the floor to hear the top two predictions from each team, asking succeeding teams to skip the predictions already made. The better course of action may be to hold off on predictions until the next morning if the network shows signs of flagging energy. This is not unusual during the first two rounds visits. The important part is for members to give predictions due consideration.

Wrapping Up

The last half hour of the day is reserved for members' reflections on the day's work. The members also generally appreciate hearing the facilitator's closing observations about their progress. Other agenda items at this time include having the facilitator remind the network about the next level of work (and possibly predictions) to be accomplished on the following day. If there is likely to be time the following morning for a short in-service, the facilitator might also pass out an article for discussion at the start of the next day. The meeting is then adjourned.

A FINAL COMMENT

There is no other way to put this: the network members will be absolutely beat at the end of the first day. The work is intellectually and emotionally demanding and requires nearly constant active participation. This is the first time many of them have ever self-consciously discussed their practice with their colleagues, and while the work is fascinating and rewarding, by the time the facilitator is summing up the day, they are ready to go home. For this reason, short and to the point are the order of the day.

CHAPTER 8

The Next Level of Work

The network should reconvene off-site the second day—the library of another school, a conference room at the central office, a room in the public library, anywhere with enough parking and private space for the morning meeting. This change in venue is important for several reasons. The network needs the privacy to speak freely, the host school staff benefit from fewer distractions off-site, and the host school needs to reclaim the space previously occupied by the network.

The members generally return upbeat and with renewed energy, having bonded over the rigors of the day before. This is all good. Part of the network's job is for members to get to know each other in this close-knit setting of hard work and speaking the truth. They will need each other in the year ahead to do the hard work of leading change in their schools and district, and for this, they will have to trust and support each other. Allow some time for chatter over coffee and baked goods, while checking in with the members of the host school to find out how they feel about the network's visit thus far. You also want to know whether their staff has given them feedback on the staff's experience with the network's visit. And if so, you should ask whether they would be willing to share it with the network during the network's forthcoming discussion on their problem of practice.

Again you have a jam-packed day, or rather, half-day. Although it seems the agenda has many items to cover, nearly everything is in service to the main thrust of the day, which is developing recommendations for the next level of work for the host school.

THE MORNING'S AGENDA

The schedule for the second day of rounds (one-half day) is outlined in exhibit 5.1 and repeated here in exhibit 8.1 for ease of reference. After a few minutes of socializing,

---

EXHIBIT 8.1

Rounds Visit Agenda

Second Day (Morning Only)

8:30–8:45	Greetings, interim feedback from host school
8:45–9:30	Follow-up in-service on questions of interest to network
9:30–10:30	Develop next level of work, including brief discussion of host school resources to address the problem of practice, the faculty sharing protocol, the strategic starting point protocol, and completion of the next level of work
10:30–10:45	Break
10:45–11:30	Teams present next level of work, questions from host school
11:30–11:40	Host school feedback to the network
11:40–11:50	Discussion with the next school to host rounds visit
11:50–12:00	Reflections from members
12:00–12:15	Session feedback process, facilitator observations, adjourn
12:15–12:45	Facilitator meets privately with host school and central office to support implementation work; release of network findings to take place as soon as possible

---

it is helpful to begin the day with a bit of in-service. The purpose of this opening forty-five-minute period is to advance network learning, but the time slot also offers flexibility as needed if the members need to catch up on unfinished work from the day before. Particularly for the first few rounds visits, the network teams sometimes need additional time to finish vetting patterns or polishing predictions.

If no extra time is needed for unfinished tasks, use the time to address questions that have come up. Facilitators can also have the members make short presentations they've prepared on a topic or can provide enrichment on related topics—for example, the latest research on new approaches to content development, new thinking around teaching, or new insights into student learning. A nice way to help the members think about next-step strategies is to have them discuss each other's school improvement work. The facilitators might open up a discussion about another school district's experience or about an issue raised by a network member, especially if the facilitator had assigned a reading on it the night before.

UPDATE ON IMPROVEMENT EFFORTS AT PREVIOUS HOST SCHOOL

This next agenda item is a brief formal, time set aside to get an update from the prior rounds host school principal, who is a month or more ahead in implementing the next level of work. Having members of the previous school report back puts them under pressure (which they sometimes need) to begin implementation. This immediate feedback also serves to inform network thinking as the members get ready for their next rounds visit. If this is the first rounds visit for the network, there will be no prior host school, but the first rounds session almost always takes longer than subsequent sessions, because of the newness of the experience.

The previous host school principal takes about five minutes to describe the steps the school has taken to act on the next-level-of-work suggestions made by network members in the previous session. The principal may also relay staff and faculty responses to the presentation of the network's patterns, as well as detail what network advice or insight had been helpful and what the network members could have done to have been more helpful. This presentation is of special interest to the current host principal, who might be wondering what it is like to begin next-step improvement ideas.

One prior host principal might say, for example, that she felt the network held back and did not go into enough detail or take a strong-enough stance on what needed to be done. She might say that she and her school can face hearing unvarnished truths and that some opportunity might have been missed in this regard.

Another principal might say his staff had difficulty making a connection between a couple of the rounds patterns and his school's problem of practice, say, around improving the students' habits of mind. He might also note that the faculty thought that a couple of the network's patterns that dealt with the content of assignments and in-class department assessments of student work missed the school's problem of practice. Such complaints can lead to productive discussions about whether the patterns were indeed connected to this problem of practice.

Of course, feedback can express both concerns and plaudits. Here are some feedback examples that express concern about the network's next level of work:

- "My next-level-of-work group talked in generalities and had problems concretely connecting the work to deliverables."
- "How are we as a district going to use our learning for a paradigm shift that teachers can understand?"
- "The next level of work requires connected teamwork, which my assistant principal will need to support. I'd love to be coached through this."

The following examples are more confident responses to the recommendations:

- "We have a real focus and determination to make changes to schools in our network."
- "My staff has responded very well to the next level of work. High-level, professional dialogue has transpired in the short time since, enabling me to develop as an instructional leader."
- "This will help other projects we are currently working on."

FOCUSING ON THE HOST SCHOOL

After getting the previous host school's feedback on the next level of work, the network now begins to make similar recommendations for the host school. The goal is to make next-level-of-work recommendations that address the school's problem of practice and that are based on the pattern statements created the day before. Again, certain steps and protocols in this next-level-of-work process will help the network members to be as detailed and concrete as possible.

The Host School's Current Resources for Problem of Practice

But before the network begins exploring how to draft the next level of work, the members need to hear what the current host school has already tried. The network members from the host school outline the school's current initiatives for addressing its problem of practice: a new math curriculum, perhaps, if the school was struggling with low math scores. The other network members may ask how the math program is progressing and what kinds of other resources (math coaches, etc.) the school might have available. They may wish to know whether those teaching math have collaborative prep time to discuss curriculum content and student progress, whether these teachers get help from a math curriculum coordinator or another specialist, or whether there are other forms of support already in place (or missing). The members will need to know all this before they can draw up suggestions of their own. This discussion is not unlike the principal's initial presentation during the preobservation meeting the day before. Only this time, the questions come from the network members, who now have specific queries based on their classroom observations—questions that anticipate having to make recommendations. Whatever the school has been doing has not worked, and the network must be creative. In helping keep network questions focused on the available resources and what has already been done, facilitators should beware of extended debates with host school representatives who feel the need to defend their prior efforts.

Exclusion of Host School Members from Next-Level-of-Work Discussions

As the midsized teams begin the work at their tables, the facilitator invites the host school members to leave their groups and become listeners-at-large. The other team members need to feel free to explore all ideas for addressing the school's problem of practice without concern for the reactions of their host school colleagues. At the same time, the host school members might have trouble being objective in devising a plan of action for their school or might be unable to resist nixing ideas they consider impractical or undoable. Such naysaying is not helpful; so-called unworkable solutions are not always unworkable. The idea here is to creatively craft solutions independent of host school thinking.

THE IMPORTANCE OF SPECIFICITY IN THE NEXT LEVEL OF WORK

In *Instructional Rounds*, City and her coauthors describe the next level of work in preparing to improve learning at scale as "the equivalent of effective lesson plans for school leaders." These plans target the problem of practice and provide clear steps the school or district could follow next week, next month, and over the course of a year. The more concrete the plans, the better. Schools need advice on specific actions they can take to improve specific practices with clearly defined resources and support.

Benefits for Everyone

Even though the host school is the focus for the recommendations, all the members learn from this work. The members should make these recommendations with the same investment they might make if they were talking about their own school. Building a sense that "we're all in this together" is an important part of creating a network community of shared practice that keeps the members dedicated, forthright, and inspired by the hope that together, they can bring about change.

As a veteran elementary school principal in the open-enrollment Cambridge Public Schools described the rounds experience, "we understand each other's struggles better. We respect each other's work more. We see the work as ours, not 'mine,' as a result of our network."

What to Consider in the Next Level of Work

As facilitator, you need to be aware that the members will find drawing up recommendations for the next level of work challenging. It is much easier to write vague suggestions—like "Do an in-service on Bloom's Revised Taxonomy" or "Bring in an expert on differentiated instruction"—and call it a day. Members often forget to make sure that their recommendations meet the following criteria:

- Reflect all the elements of the teacher, student, and content instructional core
- Address the problem of practice
- Deal with both the technical and the even-more-important adaptive changes necessary for this work to make a difference
- Confront the need for support and organizational change

It often helps to quiz each team about how its plan explicitly addresses each of these factors. The struggle to keep an eye on these elements can be learning moments and the basis for noteworthy journal entries.

Participants may find it helpful to refer to a rubric based on research by the National Council of Teachers of Mathematics (see "The Instructional Core Analysis Framework" in appendix F). This framework shows the interaction of the three elements of the instructional core in classroom dynamics. Based on earlier work that describes teaching and learning in mathematics, the framework is adapted here to apply to all subject matter areas.

The instructional core analysis framework is based on classroom observation notes recorded from sixty classrooms that describe over five hundred distinct teaching and learning episodes. Teaching and learning interaction were coded and categorized into four components: (A) questioning, (B) explaining content thinking (subject matter), (C) source of content ideas, and (D) responsibility for learning.

The framework establishes a hierarchy of four levels of classroom interaction. Level 0 describes a traditional teacher-directed classroom with brief student responses. The framework progresses to level 3, a classroom in which the teacher is coteacher and colearner, embracing meaningful collaboration for both teacher and students.

Just as a hierarchy of thinking levels detailed in Bloom's Revised Taxonomy helps members organize observation data into patterns for useful analysis and recommendations for the next level of work, so too does the instructional core analysis framework. The differences in the cognitive demand and roles of the student and teacher in classroom interactions defined in level 0 and level 3 are significant, yet the transition from one level to the next is broken down into increments so small that it is encouraging to those interested in creating change.

See exhibit 8.2 for a list of guidelines for what participants should keep in mind in crafting the next level of work.

Weekly, Monthly, and Longer Time Frames

The recommendations made in these improvement plans need to include an implementation timeline broken down into what should be accomplished by next week, by next month, and over the course of a year. While all timeframes can be difficult, members have found it especially challenging to be realistic in their long-term estimates of the amount of time required to implement successful change.

When the members are unable to come to consensus on the strategic importance of multiple recommendations under consideration by their team, the result is often a hodgepodge of suggestions. Most often, they create plans that take much longer to implement than what might be accomplished in nine months.

EXHIBIT 8.2

Guidelines for the Next Level of Work

- Identify what the school and teachers need to know and be able to do to improve learning.
- Make recommendations grounded in patterns and predictions.
- Create causal links between the recommendations and the problem of practice.
- Make transparent connections between the next level of work and all the elements of the instructional core.
- Provide details about the resources and adaptive work required to support implementation at the school and network levels.
- Outline the specific steps to be taken next week, next month, and over the course of a year.
- Generate creative, original ideas that have value.

Planning specifics by week, month, and year presents more challenges than the teams have time to solve in one morning, not to mention during a one-day rounds agenda. Nonetheless, this work is a critical next step toward implementation of what is learned from rounds. This is one reason facilitators check in periodically with the host schools over the long term. In any case, with these problems in mind, I will go over what facilitators can do to make this work more feasible. We will look at protocols for breaking the work into these week-long, month-long, and year-long components.

A WEEKLY TIME FRAME

The first step in the network's work on helping the host school resolve its problem of practice begins when the network makes recommendations for the principal to present the pattern statements to faculty and staff. What inevitably must take place in the next week at the host school is informing the faculty and staff what was seen by the network in the classrooms. Facilitators frame this network task with this question: "What would you recommend the host school do next week?"

There are many ways to accomplish this, but in light of my experience with networks of multiple sizes and configurations, I suggest that networks consider recommending the method of introducing patterns to the faculty through a specific protocol (the faculty sharing protocol, described below). This protocol can be modified or augmented by the network as it sees best.

Even with this approach, the presentation of patterns can be a stressful experience for principals concerned about faculty reaction or their ability to clearly explain the network's findings. Network recommendations for how to go about this approach can help. Many host principals appreciate help from facilitators or other network members who may be invited to be on hand when the principal makes these presentations to the school. (This is up to individual principals to request.)

The Faculty Sharing Protocol

The protocol is covered here because this is generally what networks decide to recommend for the next week's work. The purpose of the faculty sharing protocol, as designed by Australian regional network leader Mark Anderson from the Gippsland Regional Schools, is to share the network findings with the faculty members, to assure them that the findings are neither a rating nor an evaluation, and to emphasize that it is up to the schools themselves to decide on a course of action. The

THE NEXT LEVEL OF WORK

protocol's aim is to educate and create a forum in which the faculty can be brought on board through ensuring understanding first and feedback second. See exhibit 8.3 for a rundown of the protocol's steps.

Meet First with the Leadership Team

Before convening the faculty meeting, it usually helps for the principal to first share the patterns with the school's internal rounds leadership team, the same group that met with the facilitator at the pre-rounds host school meeting to help establish the school's problem of practice. This group is charged with assisting the principal in leading the implementation of the school improvement recommendations. The

---

EXHIBIT 8.3

The Faculty Sharing Protocol

1. The principal convenes the faculty meeting to present the rounds pattern statements.

2. The principal gives a brief introduction to instructional rounds and describes the process of rounds visits, emphasizing their objective, nonjudgmental focus on building a picture of teaching and learning around the school's problem of practice.

3. The principal reviews each pattern statement one by one and clarifies as necessary.

4. The principal asks the faculty members to discuss each pattern with table groups and classify them according to the following questions:

   A. What patterns do you agree with?

   B. What patterns do you question?

   C. What patterns require additional explanation or information?

   D. What patterns would you like to explore further?

5. The principal solicits and displays the table-group decisions and invites discussion, with special attention to statements grouped in the last category.

6. Faculty responses are collected and collated for later further discussion when the school is deciding on the next level of work.

members should help the principal prepare for the faculty meeting and be prepared to assist during the meeting if needed.

At the Meeting

As faculty members enter the meeting, they are handed printed copies of the network's findings and asked to sit in table groups for discussion. The principal (or
other network member) opens by briefly describing the rounds process for developing the patterns. Second, the principal should clarify pattern meanings, but not
attempt to defend or justify them. Patterns are described as snapshots of what was
seen, in light of the school's chosen problem of practice.

After all questions are satisfied, table groups of four to seven faculty are asked
to discuss the patterns and come to consensus about assigning each pattern to one
of four categories. (A pattern may be listed in more than one category, with an
explanatory note.) The categories are defined by the following questions:

1. What patterns do you agree with?
2. What patterns do you question?
3. What patterns require additional explanation or information?
4. What patterns would you like to explore further?

A scribe is chosen at each table to record the consensus results and then to
report the results aloud, category by category, when called upon by the principal. A
running tally of these results is displayed for all to see, as the first category, second,
third, and fourth begin to be filled with patterns. (Later, after the meeting is over,
these table group classifications are collected and collated for further consideration, with hard results reported back to faculty at a later date.)

Once this part of the meeting is finished, the principal asks the assembly what
understanding can be gained from what the patterns have to say about the school's
problem of practice. It may even be possible for the participants at this meeting to
come to agreement on patterns the faculty would like to explore further. The principal may find that patterns of particular interest are a good place for the school to
begin the next level of work.

Involving Faculty in the Work

The resulting entire-faculty discourse is a critical piece of the rounds process. One
of the network's objectives in making near-term recommendations for the "next
week" is to engage the entire school community in structured discourse around

specific student learning problems at the school. Recommending methods that give the faculty members a sense that they are heard and have input and control gets them actively involved as an adult learning community in the questions of how to address student learning.

The faculty tends to list most patterns in the first category—patterns that they accept and agree with. Patterns that fall into the second and third groups—patterns that are questioned and not understood—are worth further investigation.

Objecting to Patterns

In one example of registering an objection, a faculty member disagreed with a pattern statement that said boys were called upon more than girls. (It is intriguing, but not uncommon, that faculty takes exception to carefully documented tallies.) After this objection, the internal rounds leadership team decided that the school, represented by the leadership team and other interested teachers, should make its own determination by revisiting classrooms to gather data independent of the network. The school did this, with the same result.

This pattern also bothered network members from other schools so greatly that between rounds sessions, many members gathered evidence on the gender tallies of students called upon in their own schools. Again, and to their great astonishment, they got the same results. Sometimes an objection to a pattern arises from an emotional reaction, as this case points out. Educators have a sense that gender equity and fairness in classrooms is necessary, and a pattern that provides evidence to the contrary draws an immediate (in this case unfounded) rejection. Rounds opens the door to consider such issues of practice that may be so ingrained there is no way to surface them other than through the specific and nonjudgmental observation used in rounds. It is often fruitful to explore patterns that are met with objection.

The Value of Patterns That Need Exploring

Faculty responses to the fourth question (what patterns would you like to explore further?) are invaluable to school improvement efforts. It takes just one pattern deemed important to spark faculty motivation for targeted school improvement. Regardless of the chosen pattern, work on it unveils a web of interactions within the instructional core. These interactions inevitably connect to other patterns and possibly network-wide problems. The feedback resulting from the use of the faculty sharing protocol can often reshape problems of practice.

In one case, a school concerned about how well the students were able to express themselves through writing realized that its pattern analysis had broader and more serious implications. The school discovered that it had greater problems with how well the students were able to express their thinking. As a result, it expanded its problem of practice to all content areas and revised its school improvement plan accordingly.

Delay of Presentations Because of Principal's Concern About Faculty Reaction

If I see a principal delaying the faculty presentation or deciding to present only a selected group of patterns, I conclude that the principal is having trouble facing his or her staff. In cases like these, facilitators should be a bit more proactive in offering support.

To keep an eye on this, at the conclusion of each rounds session, the facilitator should ask when the principal will share the network's pattern statements and should offer support for the presentation. Internal facilitators are better positioned to anticipate potential reluctance among principals, but are at a bigger disadvantage to urge these leaders forward. If a principal is hesitant from lack of confidence, self-disclosing this to internal facilitators might be difficult. Internal facilitators may also feel awkward about pressing the matter, because of their working relationship with the principal.

When principals present a limited selection of the total number of patterns to the faculty, it may reveal either a lack of courage on the principal's part (the principal wants to control certain aspects of the school improvement process) or low expectations of the faculty's ability to take on the work, and should be discussed. But the principal's involvement in the rounds process in the first place implies a commitment to action. Facilitators can provide follow-up by early on dedicating an agenda item on the second day of every rounds visit, when the prior host principal checks in by reporting on where his or her school is acting on network suggestions or on their own plans. The network is always interested in hearing about faculty and staff reactions to the patterns. Faculty feedback from host schools informs the work of the network going forward. The network can revise its practice, including its personal leadership practice, in light of this kind of information. As mentioned above, when schools volunteer to host, they implicitly agree to assist network learning by acting on network findings and providing feedback back to the network.

A MONTHLY TIME FRAME

If the first step involves the network's recommendation that the host school principal share patterns with the faculty, the next has a more ambitious focus and requires significant creative work from the network. Network recommendations for the next month are based on the picture presented by the patterns and predictions, compared with what would be taking place if the problem of practice were solved. This means the gap between the teaching and learning currently taking place in the classroom and the kind of teaching and learning you would like to see. Bridging the gap will require more than one school year to solve, but begins with the first month and moves month by month and then year by year.

The Strategic Starting Point Protocol

Because the idea of coming up with suggestions on a month-by-month time frame can often overwhelm networks, confusing the members about which recommendations might be strategic, many members, as mentioned, try a shotgun approach to cover all possibilities. To help them through this process, I developed something I call the strategic starting point protocol. It structures a fifteen-minute discussion to jump-start network action on leadership lesson planning. Once a team agrees on a specific place to begin, the development of lesson plans and the resolve for action gain momentum.

In this protocol, the midsized teams of the network are asked to imagine themselves in the role of host school leadership trying to decide a strategic starting point from which to launch the work in the next month. (At this point, they have no idea how the host school faculty might actually weigh in on this question, because the faculty has yet to see the patterns, so the members should not waste time trying to guess.)

The strategic starting point protocol structures network thinking around next-level-of-work recommendations for the host school for longer time frames—next month and over the next year. The protocol helps guide members who may be stuck on deciding where to start this work. It provides structure by requiring the members to think within a realistic framework and forces them to explain their rationale for recommendations. It ends up generating more-creative plans than might otherwise result.

This protocol requires members to choose a starting point that will root the first month's lesson plan in purposeful action. No lesson plans are formulated yet. See exhibit 8.4 for an outline of the process, which is spelled out in more detail below.

EXHIBIT 8.4

Strategic Starting Point Protocol

1. Ask the host school principal to identify the amount of staff meeting time (faculty, grade-level, leadership meetings) as well as the school resources that are available for working on recommendations.

2. Give the team members fifteen minutes to decide on a body of work on which lesson plans for the first month can be created to respond to the host school's problem of practice.

3. Have the members present and explain their ideas to the network before they begin to write detailed lesson plans based on their chosen starting point.

The facilitator begins by asking the host principal to detail what staff meeting time is available for beginning the improvement efforts over the next month. Specifically, ask how many faculty, grade-level, and leadership-team meetings held in the next month can be devoted to rounds follow-up. This next-month time period is the month following the meeting at which the principal introduces the pattern statements to the faculty and staff at the school.

Networks need to know the exact amount of time available to conceive of realistic starting points. Time constraints severely limit school leadership action, a reality that network discussions about starting points must live with.

Now ask the table groups to assume they can use the time detailed by the principal, say, a typical one-hour faculty meeting and a one-hour department or grade-level meeting, to address the problem of practice in light of the network findings. Ask where they would start in that first block of time. In what area and with what specific focus would they base their lesson plans on? If there is only one hour of faculty meeting time available next month, the starting point is of strategic importance.

Teams are allotted fifteen minutes to agree on a strategic starting point. They assign a scribe to keep notes. No leadership lesson plans are written yet because this is an introductory discussion, but their choices will serve as the basis for the leadership lesson plans they will be developing.

Facilitators should encourage the teams to be creative. The more variations in starting points, the better for generating alternative school options. Team participants find this work fascinating as they become keenly interested in and debate what their peers think and why. There are no right answers, and of course, one-hour faculty meetings solve no problems. The availability of school meeting times presents a sobering context for big ideas about closing the gap between current practice and resolution of the school's problem of practice.

After fifteen minutes, each team presents its idea for a starting point. The team spokesperson should be asked to explain what starting point was chosen and why. It is just as instructive to the network to hear about starting points not chosen and why.

Here is one example: If the school's problem of practice is "students taking responsibility for their own learning," one team may decide that the school should start on the practice of question asking, with a faculty meeting, for example, discussing the purposes of questions or the student's role in question asking. Another team may decide that the school should focus on student engagement, while a third may decide to focus on increasing the student voice in the classroom.

Each team then explains why it chose the proposed starting point. Each proposal has pros and cons, yet all proposals merit consideration. It is a tremendous resource to the host school when each team recommends a different starting point, increasing the school's possible options for attacking its problem of practice. This ends the protocol.

The facilitator then asks each team to flesh out its recommendations in detail as described below, using the strategic starting point it decided on. In this way, the team creates a bank of ideas (lesson plans) with alternative ways of going about the work useful to all, not just the host school.

LONGER TIME FRAMES: OVER THE NEXT MONTH TO A PLAN FOR THE YEAR

The final steps in making recommendations for the school's next level of work require the teams to describe detailed meeting agendas with lesson-plan specificity for the next month and, in less detail, for the next nine months. These are less recommendations for the school to implement than a smorgasbord of options it could employ, with clarity about objectives, involving each element of the instructional core.

Team suggestions should account for the realistic utilization of resources, the technical skills required for instructional practice, the role of leadership, and the organizational support required to improve learning at scale. These plans address what teachers and the school should know and be able to do to improve learning, as well as what needs to happen within the district for these efforts to succeed.

When Plans Become Too General

Facilitators should watch carefully. Often as many as half the teams announce prematurely that they are finished when they lay down their lesson plans for the next month. You should therefore monitor team progress as they near completion to see whether a full nine months have been addressed. The plans for the months following the first are not expected to be in as great detail, but they should clearly convey what is recommended to be done and why. Early finishers can be asked to provide more comprehensive detail. Only when they've outlined the full nine months should they post their lesson plans on the walls. As this work progresses over many rounds, the members find it easier to take the full scope of the work into account, with many using electronic devices to look up research and citing specific resources to add to their plans.

Obviously, the timing of rounds visits within the school calendar year influences planning for the next level of work. Rounds visits held in September require different planning than those held in May, even though the next level of work should always include nine months of planning. Ask the members to incorporate the intervening variables such as summer vacation and the start of a new school year as opportunities to advance the work. Commitment to change must be enduring, and the intervening variables within the nine-month parameter are realities that can be accounted for and used as opportunities.

PRESENTING THE NEXT LEVEL OF WORK

Upon team completion of these recommendations, plans are committed to poster paper for display and presentation. Two audiences await: their peer teams and the intently waiting host school members.

As the team members describe and provide justification for their ideas, the host school principal and colleagues listen and take notes, sometimes asking for elaboration. Presentations are for clarity, not debate. Host school members should make sure they understand as much as possible. They will not be deciding on any one plan at this point. They will do that on another day, when they have had more time. They will want to wait in any case until after they have shared and discussed the patterns with the faculty. They can also decide to devise a separate plan of their own. The recommendations for the next level of work should be regarded as possibilities, not working papers. Still, we expect the school to act upon network findings, and whatever the school decides to do to resolve its problem of practice, the approach will differ from what the school has done before.

Network Member Principals Reluctant to Advise Their Host School Peers

It is not uncommon in this session for some network principals to express reluctance about advising their host school colleague. They may not mind sharing their own experience, but most find it hard to tell another principal what to do. This is a holdover from past practices, but can be deeply ingrained in some individuals and stand in the way of free discussions about the next level of work. Interestingly, teachers and central office personnel have little compunction making recommendations to principals, despite the seeming taboo for colleague principals to do so.

Continually remind the network members that the next level of work provides options, not orders. Creative, informed ideas serve as a rich resource for the host schools as well as for everyone else present. It is up to the school to decide the value of the ideas generated in the next level of work.

Releasing the Documents to the Host School

Immediately after the conclusion of the second day of rounds, the facilitators will release the three products of the rounds process—the pattern statements, the predictions, and the recommendations for the next level of work—to the host school principal. The network members are usually also interested in receiving copies of their work for their own records.

To enable the flexible use by the host school (and the network) and ease in interpretation, the district clerical assistant prepares these products as three separate documents from each midsized team, with the date, host school name, and midsized team designation at the top of each page. For example, if there were six observation teams, there would be three midsized teams and nine documents in all. The midsized team document headings would be as follows: Team 1 and 2; Team 3 and 4; and Team 5 and 6. They are listed in this way for each set of patterns, for example, so that the school can gain further insight into the magnitude of the problem of practice. If all three midsized teams find exactly the same pattern, such as "Recall and understanding questions are asked by teachers," it is clear that the pattern is a predominant one. The way in which patterns are similar or vary from one team to the next may help the school reflect on its problem of practice. Since the predictions and next level of work also arise from the work of each set of team patterns, the team-designation header linking the three documents, team by team, identifies how each team progressed through its work. Each stage of the rounds process is based upon the prior stage of the work, and without team designations, this might be difficult to trace from beginning to end. Host schools understand network findings better when they can follow the progression from patterns to the next level of work team by team.

Delivering work products at the end of the second day allows the host school principal to immediately begin to process the organized, objective information before progressing to the next step of discussing the results with faculty. Facilitators should release these results to the principal as soon as possible to capitalize on this keen interest in the hope of encouraging implementation, as well as to empower the principal to provide instructional leadership as a result of his or her rounds experience. It is up to the principal to decide how to present the material to the faculty. Of course, the expectation is that the faculty will be interested in and discuss the patterns among themselves and the building staff. Many principals hold off on presenting the next level of work until due consideration is given to the patterns and predictions. Even then the principal may decide to use the next-level-of-work documents as a personal resource to keep in mind as the school develops its own next level of work.

The network and facilitators never deal directly with faculty on the findings (that is, unless some faculty members belong to the network or unless the principal invites the facilitator or, better yet, a network colleague to the faculty meeting for support). Once the job of hosting this rounds visit is over, the principal and the rest of the school leadership are in charge of leading the improvement efforts. The roles of the network and facilitators at this point are simply to support the principal's efforts.

FINAL AGENDA ITEMS: REFLECTIONS AND FEEDBACK

After dedicating a full rounds session to examining the host school's problem of practice, observing, screening evidence, finding patterns, making predictions, and now, offering an array of possible ways to address the problem, network members thank the host school principal for volunteering and settle back to receive his or her thoughts on the experience of hosting the network. This is just an early reaction and more about the rounds process than about the network's findings about the school, since the principal has yet to run the patterns past the faculty.

Presentation by Upcoming Host School Principal

It is now time to hear a couple words from the next principal to host the next month's rounds visit. Keep in mind that you as facilitator should already have completed a visit to this upcoming host school to help finalize its problem of practice, assisted the principal in the preparation of these remarks, toured the school, and so forth. Even though the school may still be refining its problem of practice, a brief sketch can be helpful, along with a quick word covering practical matters such as parking and the like.

Final Reflections

Facilitators now review the hard work of the past two days by noting how the network members have grown since the launch session and how the members should strive to improve their work on the next rounds. This is also the time to give homework readings or other assignments to acquaint the members with some recent research or to share resources for activities that can be used on the job to further the work. Finally, facilitators may need to schedule a think-tank meeting sometime before the next rounds session.

Before the group breaks up, the members complete a session feedback form (see exhibit 4.6). The results can be sent by email or shared at the beginning of the next rounds meeting. Once the members complete the survey, they are free to go.

Host School Follow-Up

Facilitators stay behind for a thirty-minute private meeting with a central office representative and host school members. Open the conversation by inviting the host school members to share any further thoughts on the rounds visit along with concerns they may have moving forward. You also discuss their upcoming faculty pattern presentation and ask whether the principal feels confident in using the faculty sharing protocol or wishes to take another route. Explore what other kinds of support they might find useful.

ONGOING WORK

The session is over, but the facilitator's work continues. You will need to think about how to support host school needs; set aside time to debrief the experience with your cofacilitator (if you have one); help the next host school develop its problem of practice and prepare for its rounds visit; perhaps meet with the think tank; and prepare the next agenda and related in-service to move the network forward.

PART 4

From Implementation
to Improvement

CHAPTER 9

The Theory of Action and Beyond

This forward-looking phase of instructional rounds work is the focus of this chapter and takes place months after the first rounds visit. Network members now have maybe three rounds visits behind them and are becoming comfortable with the language, the process, and each other. You'll notice they're more confident about strategizing for classroom visits, more objective in what they see, better listeners of disparate points of view, and more straightforward in discussing their thinking. They are also noticeably more relaxed and trusting about challenging each other in discussion. Importantly, they are beginning to feel common ownership for this change. When members talk about "our students" and moving the work into classrooms district-wide, you know they are ready for the personal accountability and formal commitment demanded by writing their own theories of action.

As described in *Instructional Rounds*, a theory of action is a conditional statement that captures the essential connections between a leader's practice and what happens in classrooms. Network members write their own theory of action when they gain enough experience to conduct a comprehensive analysis of a problem of practice and develop equally reflective recommendations about what to do about it for the next level of work. Periodic feedback from the host schools on the viability of network recommendations helps the network members gain a sense of what can be realistically accomplished within the time frame of a school year. This informs their thinking as they begin composing a theory of action for their own work. For this, we convene a special interim network session.

THE INTERIM NETWORK SESSION

Interim sessions are held at midpoint between rounds sessions and at the end of the year to refocus and establish goals for forthcoming work. Facilitators plan for these sessions jointly with think tank members and the network's convening authority.

These interim agendas include self-reflection—to assess how far the network members' rounds skills have come—discussion about how their professional practice has been affected by rounds work, a sharing of implementation experiences, an in-service on relevant topics of interest, and, finally, discussion on how to further implement new knowledge and refine the members' leadership practice through writing theories of action.

This chapter is about how to continuously move forward with rounds work, which includes how to write a theory of action. I'll revisit discussion of the interim network session agenda later in the chapter.

WRITING A THEORY OF ACTION

A theory of action is the writer's public written commitment to taking specific strategic actions to implement ways to improve learning. As an implementation plan and statement of intent, it shows how school leaders aim to focus their student learning improvement ambitions. This plan of action describes goals that are to be achieved through a process that includes self-chosen, measureable markers. These markers allow members to check progress on established criteria, learn from the consequences of their actions, and make corrections as necessary. Circumstances during the course of a year may force theory adjustments, in which case the documents are revisited for revision.

Theories of action statements begin, "If I [do these things or take this action], then [these measureable actions] will take place." Such statements help define the kind of leadership the writer intends to exercise in order to achieve specific results. The statements must be falsifiable, allowing one to understand when they don't work. This means writers should compose statements in such a way that the results of specific actions can be measured in order to determine whether their intentions have been achieved. The theory of action is intended to represent the writer's best-informed thinking at the time it is written; the writer understands that it will be revised as needed in response to new conditions, successes, or failures. See exhibit 9.1 for the important elements that define a theory of action.

EXHIBIT 9.1

A Theory of Action Defined

- It is an if-then proposition that captures the essential connections between the writer's practice and what happens in classrooms.
- It is falsifiable.
- It is an accurate representation of the writer's practice at this moment.
- It distinguishes the essential elements from the less important.

Leaders should always share their theory of action with school organizations to make leadership intention more visible. Even staff who may not agree with the cause-and-effect relationships described in the action document can become more willing to join in the work when they see a leader's open and straightforward statement of intent to improve student learning. When leadership actions are consistent with these statements, staff usually regard the leader as a dependable partner in improvement efforts.

A theory of action establishes criteria that help leaders recognize when new proposals and assignments distract from the plan of action. It provides justification for turning down that next great idea that seems to always be walking through the door, but that threatens to interrupt focus on the current effort. Good ideas relevant to the theory of action do come along at times and may be incorporated by the writer if they pass this test of being functionally related to the document's purpose.

Purpose of a Theory of Action

Theories of action are written by focusing on specific problems of practice anchored in the instructional core. This is why you seek problems of practice that are of consequence to both the host school and the network—they are not just to focus rounds work, but are, importantly, to move change forward. The idea is to create a plan of action for improving student learning around this problem of practice that is transparently understandable to you and others. It should be written in such a way as to allow you to track your learning over time as you implement school improvement efforts, and to guide you in focusing your energy and attention on the essential elements of the work.

Starting Out as a Group

According to *Instructional Rounds*, theories of action are best written initially as a group exercise with support from colleagues. As feelings of personal and professional safety among colleagues increase, group members are better able discuss leadership ideals and new proposals. They can speak freely of what they need to learn, seek the opinions of others, unhesitatingly question what is said, and work to change past practices and culture.

Studying Sample Theories of Action

Members find writing theories of action very challenging—it helps to read sample theories of actions before writing their drafts. Facilitators should have the members start with simplified, narrowly constructed statements that describe one strategy, before they try to cover multiple strategies with a more complex document. This is a personal approach to action, unique to the writer, and is a new way of thinking and working. The job of the facilitator is to tell them to ignore trying to be perfect (there is no such thing as a perfect theory of action) and instead to think through their leadership practice, make their best effort to state it effectively, and revise their statement (and their leadership) in light of experience. See exhibit 9.2 for several examples, all of which were revised by their authors during the first year. (Sample statements may also be found in *Instructional Rounds*.)

Of course, such theories of action are only useful to the extent that they are implemented and measurable by criteria specified within the statement. (Note that despite being defined by an ongoing series of benchmarks, because of their long time frame, theories of action are unlikely to be completely measureable or their effects completely known until the following year.)

Initially Limiting the Scope

Facilitators should ask the members to limit the scope of the first theory of action to no more than one complex sentence, since they can get overwhelmed and lose sight of their goal when they take on too much. The purpose is to learn the concept through focusing on one student improvement idea that is measurable by objective data. This should be consistent with school and district improvement plans as well.

A Vision of a Problem of Practice Solved

The formulation of a theory begins with a problem of practice generated out of school and district data. The whole point of a problem of practice is that it clearly

---

EXHIBIT 9.2

Examples of Theories of Action

From a central office leader:

If I implement a coaching program for instructional leadership with principals to enhance their ability to question and challenge teachers about the level and complexity of content and pedagogy, then improved student learning outcomes will result.

From a principal:

If I lead the implementation of improved instructional practice through pattern analysis, collaborative staff workshops, related professional development on the instructional core, discussions of specified professional readings, and the monitoring and analysis of assessment outcomes and the functioning of professional learning teams, then both staff capacity to improve student performance and student performance itself will improve.

From a principal:

If I develop the leadership team's knowledge and work jointly with it to develop staff members' understanding of the concepts of the instructional core as the basis for teaching and learning so that they can develop better planning documents that focus on learning intent and the criteria of success, then learning outcomes will improve.

From an entire network after a year of rounds:

If we build instructional leadership through the analysis of data, observation of practice, and increased knowledge of the instructional core, then we will develop an informed and purposeful school improvement process that will lead to improved outcomes for all students.

---

and concretely identifies one particular problem with student learning at the school or network level—a problem that can be addressed if understood. Seeing the problem clearly is what helps guide improvement efforts. The first step in this is to identify a broader vision of what might be seen if the problem of practice were solved and then what it would take to get there. Solving a problem of practice can take years to accomplish, which makes it important to identify only one specific area of progress that could reasonably be accomplished in one school year.

Keeping a one-year timeline in mind, members are asked to determine the strategies (technical and adaptive) needed to produce a year of progress with accompanying indicators to determine progress.

It Takes a Network

Remind the members that multiple people in their organization will be involved in implementing the strategy. Members then forecast what is required to implement their strategy, specifying job responsibilities (their own and others'), as well as estimates of the amount of time needed to accomplish this vision according to a month-by-month timeline. The timeline is important in helping writers come to terms with the reality of accounting for the relevant tangibles, such as school resources, particular job functions, and available meeting times. Theory of action statements should be far-reaching yet accomplishable if all goes well.

Taking Responsibility

Members sift through the timelines of necessary actions in order to glean which actions they themselves would need to take on. These actions serve as the basis for writing a draft theory of action, translated into the format: "If I do [these things], then [these measureable actions] will take place, and student learning will improve." Once the drafts are complete, the writers share them with their network colleagues for feedback before the drafts are finalized. See the writing guidelines in exhibit 9.3 to help members review each other's draft statements.

For feedback, each member passes his or her draft statement around the table to the right. The receiving members analyze and comment on the statement, using the checklist in exhibit 9.3. The drafts circulate until returned to their authors. The members read the comments and discuss them, then revise their drafts as needed.

How a Theory of Action Can Help Reveal Problems

An example of how a theory of action can help you become a more effective leader comes from Jeanette, a principal of a midsized high school that I was working with. During a session on assessing theories of action written six months earlier, she described how discouraged she was: "I thought through what I would do carefully. I worked six different steps into my theory of action, along with measurable ways to gauge how it was working. I knew we were going to be discussing this

---

EXHIBIT 9.3

Checklist for Evaluating a Theory of Action

The if-then proposition must meet the following criteria:

- Contain connections between the writer's professional practice and what happens in the classroom.
- Be stated in the first person.
- Account for the school's or district's problem of practice.
- Be consistent with district-targeted objectives and goals.
- Be falsifiable, allowing the writer to acknowledge when he or she is wrong.
- Distinguish essential elements from the less important ones.
- Be able to be measured in one school year.
- List specific steps or actions the authors must take to accomplish items.
- Be far-reaching, yet realistic and doable.

---

today, so last week, I took one more tour through my building to look for signs of change. I saw no change except in a couple of classrooms."

I told her that it was progress: now she knew six things that didn't work. (Without testing her theory of action, she would have continued believing she was making a difference. These results told her she would have to be more creative and stretch to try ideas she'd not tried before.)

A year and a half later, Jeanette announced to the network that following our talk eighteen months earlier, she had begun soul-searching and returned to her theory of action in which she had clearly sketched out the importance of faculty and staff in her school improvement plan. She now had to admit she wasn't sure how much she had involved them with developing and executing her plan. At her next faculty meeting, she invited candid feedback, which helped her realize she had not sufficiently invited their input into her plans for change. Once figuring it out, she said she changed the form and content of her faculty meetings and everything then seemed to fall into place. "I feel much better," she said. "Now we all see evidence of improved student learning. We may not be there yet, but we are on our way, even seeing an uptick in test scores."

Learning from Others

When I was superintendent of schools in Cambridge, Massachusetts, I found it instructive to read the action plan documents of our entire network. I gained a comprehensive understanding of what the collection of district leadership felt was important, their varying perspectives on leadership roles, how they planned to measure or gauge their progress, and their commitment to the work.

In discussing our documents and considering what revisions we needed to make, we quickly learned that our first theories of action were often overly ambitious and sometimes focused more on technical work than the adaptive work necessary for strategy implementation. Working through these challenges, we learned in a visceral way how important collegial support could be in critically assessing and revising our plans.

Sharing all of our theories allowed us to see the impact of the totality of our actions, while also enabling us to link support for each other. We began to eagerly anticipate hearing how others' theories of action were working with the hope that their successes would inform our own.

The work of striving to commit to theories that are far-reaching yet realistic and effective, while knowing there are no surefire theories, can feel quite risky. Facilitators look for ways to encourage the network members to provide each other support to take the risks involved with enacting bold, forthright leadership with the potential for significant change.

INTERIM ROUNDS MEETINGS

Interim rounds sessions are important for moving work forward from school to district in order to achieve large-scale change. The midpoint between rounds sessions and the end-of-year sessions give members a chance to step back and review the goals for their rounds work, take stock of network development, and formulate action to increase the efficacy of network aims to improve adult and student learning. The agendas are as varied as the networks and usually reflect the network's stage of development. Possible useful agenda items to consider include assessment, in-service follow-up on questions arising from previous rounds visits, and recalibration of work and goals. See exhibit 9.4 for a few sample agenda items with accompanying activities that facilitators might want to consider in one form or another.

EXHIBIT 9.4

Possible Interim Session Agenda Items

Skill development

- Replay a launch session video. Members compare current and past note taking and observation skills.
- Discuss the effectiveness of member-led table group facilitation.
- Members analyze a packet of patterns, predictions, and next level of work from prior rounds. How have skills progressed? What would improve the work?

Implementation

- Discuss the role of the instructional core in daily practice in network schools.
- Members share their experience with applying rounds work to their daily practice.
- Discuss the connection between rounds work and district and state programs and requirements.
- Looking at an analysis of all patterns, predictions, and the next-level-of-work documents, determine if there are district patterns that warrant the development of a district problem of practice.

In-service

- Present in-service topics such as feedback, research, question asking, or others of importance to the group. This in-service can be prepared in advance and presented by the members individually or as a study group, be based on articles read in advance for discussion, or employ some other method of information sharing.
- Members analyze their own school data packets to develop a problem of practice with support from colleagues.

Instructional rounds is not a program; it is a different way of working. The agenda items reflect this in focusing on how to engage the network in shared thinking and cooperative action to move the work forward.

LARGE-SCALE CHANGE: MOVING FROM SCHOOLS TO DISTRICTS

Your ultimate aim in moving your network forward is large-scale change—improving learning from individual schools to entire districts. After a year or so of doing rounds, your network should be ready to explore district-wide problems of practice based on problems it finds common among the network schools. District-wide problems of practice can also be found in district climate surveys, state test scores, and school improvement plans, in addition to within the classrooms of the schools themselves

Once a problem of practice is developed to represent the entirety of network schools within the district, network members then make rounds visits with dual problems of practice in mind: one school-based and the other district-wide. Working with two problems of practice requires greater sophistication that takes more than a few rounds sessions to develop. Like theories of action, work on district-wide problems of practice is not undertaken until the members are comfortably well into rounds work.

An Example of a District-Wide Problem of Practice

For a district-wide problem of practice in Elizabeth, New Jersey, we reviewed a two-year set of prior patterns and next-level-of-work recommendations from multiple networks in the district. The first two years of rounds yielded several consistent district-wide patterns: students were hard at work in a friendly, supportive environment, yet teacher questions and student work rarely went beyond recall and understanding; students expected to be told what to do next; and student questions were primarily procedural in nature, with an overall culture of passive compliance among students and staff. These repeated patterns led to the development of a district-wide problem of practice: "In what ways and to what extent are classroom-school-district level forces impacting cognitive demand in the instructional core and a more active role of the learner?"

This problem of practice became an ongoing part of our rounds work in addition to the individual school problems of practice we were studying. This upped the ante for all the network participants. As one central office administrator put it, "the next level of work gained immediate significance for more than just the host school." Once a host school's problem of practice is addressed through crafting patterns, predictions, and the next level of work, networks then reflect on whether anything new has been revealed that could be applied to the district's problem of practice. This results in district-wide recommendations that support and assist individual school and network progress through more systemic organizational change.

MOVING FROM LEARNING TO IMPLEMENTATION

The facilitator's job is not finished with the completion of rounds visits. It is not really over until the network determines whether the recommendations for improvement as well as personal theories of action are yielding the desired results. As facilitator, you have certainly stepped back from leading the meetings—this they can now do almost entirely themselves—but you are still needed as an independent outside voice keeping an eye on the more rigorous aspects of the process and serious follow-up: interim network meetings, follow-up visits with host schools, and continued strategizing with network and district leadership. Your extended work is aimed at helping members use the agency of the network as a resource to continually move improvement forward in an ongoing, collegial, professional practice of excellence. For some networks and districts, this work will permanently redefine the nature of educational practice.

There are many factors, however, small or otherwise, that impact this work. Let's look at some of these factors.

Engaging Teachers

This book has not said a lot about involving teachers directly in rounds work. This is partly because the focus of rounds is leadership change. But teachers are an obvious critical link to this work, and their participation in rounds work is invaluable. Teacher leaders are important rounds or faculty links, and if they are not included in the first network, arrangements should be made to include them later. Most network principals return to their schools to discuss it with faculty, but find that when teacher leaders actually participate in rounds, their increased understanding and new ways of interpreting what is happening in classrooms makes them critical partners in working with their faculty peers to improve learning in the classroom. Many of the launch session training exercises and materials and rounds protocols can be used in faculty staff meetings as a way to engage faculty in self-study and observation in each other's classrooms.

Recognizing Progress in the Members

Facilitators should frequently and privately check in with the members to ask how their rounds experience is influencing their practice. Curiously, often the first network members to begin acting on what they are learning do so quietly, without a word to their colleagues. Perhaps their reticence is a final holdover from the culture of nice, in which they fear shaming their colleagues by their own good work. In any case, if a facilitator notices that certain members have made good progress, it is a good idea to ask them to share their progress and what they have learned at the next in-service meeting.

Measuring Progress

A necessary feature of long-term rounds work is an end-of-year assessment. Year-to-year comparisons of district and school data can be a useful component. In Cambridge, when we set out to improve student math performance, we used the state tests as one barometer of our progress.

Another way to measure network member growth is to devise your own survey (perhaps using SurveyMonkey or another electronic survey instrument), asking members to complete it at the end of the year. The collated, anonymous results provide candid feedback that promotes healthy discussion and ideas for improving network functioning.

Addressing the Question "When Do We Start?"

Be alert for opportunities to move the network to action. During one of my rounds sessions in Australia, Bob, a principal in the forty-member network, announced, "We've been learning a lot, including myself, and we all talk about how so many things in our schools should be different. I thought something was going to be done about it, but I don't see anything happening."

Apparently Bob, though willing, thought applying what was learned was someone else's responsibility. To give the work back to the person who asks this sort of question, facilitators can ask, "So, what is holding you back? When are you going to do something about it?"

The discussion that followed resulted in a network decision to ask the think tank to develop a list of individual and network options for action, with the ideas and action that followed proving effective at moving implementation plans forward. Discussions of desire to change the status quo is an indication that it is time to write an initial theory of action. Had they already done so in this case, Bob would have had no reason to raise the question, because all the participants would have been actively working on implementation through their theories of action.

ACCOUNTABILITY

The culture of accountability developed through instructional rounds work is not based on authority relationships; instead, it is about encouraging the participants to think and act as network members who recognize the importance of shared accountability for improving professional practice and learning outcomes. The kind of observation and analysis employed in a disciplined rounds process creates a strong, visible culture of instructional practice to improve both adult and student learning.

By measuring achievement of their stated outcomes, productive theories of action enable their authors to determine whether their professional practice is effective. The authors are accountable to themselves and their network colleagues in working together to improve learning at scale. The link within the rounds network process to accountability is based upon the principle of reciprocity, which states that "for every increment of performance I demand from you, I have an equal responsibility to provide you with the capacity to meet that expectation. Likewise, for every investment you make in my skill and knowledge, I have a reciprocal responsibility to demonstrate some new increment of performance" (Richard F. Elmore, *Bridging the Gap Between Standards and Achievement: The Imperative for Professional Development in Education* [Washington, DC: Albert Shanker Institute, 2002], 5).

Many network members find it difficult to hold each other accountable to their stated commitments to student learning and self-improvement. Much of this aspect of network functioning is covered in the drawing up of network norms. The difficulties networks experience are cause for think-tank action, and the network's adopted norms must often be reconsidered and revised so that they become more functional. Nonetheless, it is often something that networks struggle with. The following discussion looks at a few accountability issues that commonly come up.

The Role of Superintendents

As always, superintendents should continuously check in with host school principals to discuss their progress and what further support they could use. The districts themselves also need to be assessed and should be listed on the agenda of the end-of-year meeting to report on what is being done district-wide to extend, support, and capitalize on the host school's efforts. The efficacy of the network depends on district-wide organizational change. Network members should not forget to stand back and look at this.

Superintendents Who Worry About Micromanaging

Sometimes, when network participants don't seem to be acting on what they were learning, I take the district superintendent aside to discuss the issue. In one case, a superintendent (who was a network member) expressed discomfort at telling his principals what to do. He felt the members were not committed to making the necessary changes, but was reluctant to speak up because he felt it would make things uncomfortable politically if he tried to supervise their actions. We solved the problem by requiring all the members to commit to a theory of action in which they declared their intentions for future action. The superintendent's job then involved making sure the theories were consistent with district goals so that his checking in had more to do with checking on the progress they were making.

A Theory of Action Is Not an Evaluation Instrument

A theory of action is not a gotcha document to be used against individuals; it is instead a leadership development instrument. Leaders who write theories of action are expected (with district support) to follow through on them, and if they fail to do so, their fellow network members should support, prod, and hold the leaders accountable. Members are also accountable to the person who supervises them. Supervisors should not hesitate to evaluate implementation follow-through and the revision process on a theory, but not whether a far-reaching goal has been immediately achieved, since the documents are designed to encourage risk taking and learning from mistakes. If supervisors need to conduct evaluations, there are many other ways to do so instead of using the writer's achievement of a personal theory of action against them.

How to Create a Culture of Accountability

Accountability begins with the network's development of norms. Empowering an ad hoc think tank in the development of norms is the first step, and the ongoing work of a more permanent think tank guiding council is next. The facilitator's goal in cultivating think-tank members is for them to assume greater and greater responsibility for the functioning of the network as a collegial body founded on shared responsibility. The focus is always on whether learning is improving at scale across the network. This work involves identifying what actions are yielding improvement, what is hindering progress, and what is the next step for the network. This means that members hold each other accountable, individually and collectively, for the implementation and the ultimate efficacy of the work.

The following account illustrates how some network members, in this case, three principals, struggled to make sense of rounds work. For these three principals, it ultimately had to be the network who set them right.

An Example of a Struggle to Implement a Course of Action

In working with a network in a large school system, I once had three host school principals who had set out to reverse patterns of inadequate student learning by engaging their leadership teams and district staff developers to assist in committing to a course of action.

Their course of action focused on increasing the level of challenge and deepening student learning in the classroom. The data patterns had demonstrated that student work across their schools was primarily recall and understanding; that student responses on assignments were primarily one-word answers; and that teacher tolerance of student errors was minimal. In addition, when students were unable to answer questions, rather than help students learn what they didn't know, teachers either called on other students or answered the question themselves.

These principals began work on the problem by first sharing network findings with faculty and then developing action plans that began with in-service on Bloom's Revised Taxonomy or Costa's Levels of Thinking. They arranged for teachers to observe each other, held faculty meetings to share and model higher-order questions and assignments, and convened grade-level meetings to incorporate key questions in teacher lesson plans. As the principals reported at later rounds sessions, questions had even been written into lesson plans reflecting an elevated challenge to solicit deeper student thinking. They were so certain of the efficacy of their interventions, they generously shared their action plans on visits to a new host school with similar problems.

The problem, however, was they had yet to see improvement. Facilitators need to raise questions if they encounter situations like this. In my own situation, I asked the team of principals, "When you visit your classrooms, do you see teachers asking higher-order questions and students demonstrating deeper thinking?"

"No," conceded one. "I saw some change at first, but now I have to say that I don't see much."

When I asked why he had made recommendations to others when they had yet to see the improvements they hoped for, the principal hesitated. All three principals then confirmed they and their leadership teams saw no major change when visiting classrooms informally or during walkthroughs.

This is when the next question (one the principals had been reluctant to ask themselves) is "Why not?" This is always the network's job—or at the beginning, the facilitator's—to encourage investigation and reconsideration of professional practice even in the face of member discomfort.

After some hesitation, the answers came. All three principals emphasized that the teachers understood what was expected and that most knew how to do it. The technical skills needed for asking higher-order questions were not at issue; the teachers were on board with the importance of elevating cognitive demand and achieving conceptual understanding. But the teachers reported that questions on district benchmark tests, given frequently in multiple subject areas throughout the year, were primarily recall and understanding, not conceptual understanding or application. Teachers confessed they felt caught in a bind between the need to increase both cognitive demand and conceptual understanding and the need to keep up with the pacing guides for covering material for the next test.

This story reveals that instructional rounds pushes on many points in the system: not only individual teachers but also curriculum planners, principals, and superintendents. In the face of pressure on test scores, schools and district leaders need to advocate strongly for a laser-like focus on instruction. The rounds network in this particular district recognized this and went on to develop a problem of practice that investigated the pressures that inhibited efforts to increase rigor and engagement in the classroom.

HOW THE CAMBRIDGE PUBLIC SCHOOLS IMPROVED

To finish the story I began in the introduction, I came to this work as superintendent of a troubled urban school district in Cambridge. For several decades, the Cambridge Public Schools spent more per pupil than nearly all other school districts in the state. In fact, of the twenty-five school districts labeled by the state's Department of Education as "urban" (defined as having comparatively high levels of poverty and high numbers of English language learners and minority students),

Cambridge spent far more per pupil than others in the urban cohort—in many cases twice as much. Cambridge's student demographics placed the school system in the middle of the urban cohort, and embarrassingly to me, so too did the student state test scores. Simply put, the demographics—and not the amount of spending, supposedly for better education—predicted performance.

Despite expenditures of more than $20,000 per pupil, there was no evidence that these extraordinary expenditures yielded extraordinary results in student learning. By 2003, the state Education Management Audit Council (EMAC) had initiated on-site examinations for past poor student performance and placed the school district on watch status.

Despite this bad news, as the new superintendent in 2003, I felt that the district had a rare opportunity to change the lives of an urban student population so much in need of a great education. When one day, after a superintendent's seminar at the Harvard University School of Education, I asked Richard Elmore about his leadership rounds sessions, I had no idea the impact this would have on the Cambridge schools (as well as on my professional life). When our district leadership formed the Cambridge Leadership Network to implement instructional rounds, we were fortunate to have three exceptional facilitators in our first two years: Richard Elmore, Elizabeth City, and Sarah Fiarman of the Harvard team.

Forming the Cambridge Leadership Network

Over the next several years, the entire administrative team, from superintendent and central office administrators to principals, devoted two to three days each month on instructional rounds. The Harvard team knew that we, not the facilitators, had to do the hard work and find answers to our own questions. They pushed us to pursue deeper learning and to take responsibility for running the network itself. They did not hesitate to ask probing questions about our follow-up work on rounds. They called attention to critical evidence, pressing us to act on it. We found that the shared culture of leadership, improved professional practice, and the impact of a common language soon found their way into our daily working relationships, our decision making at all levels, and ultimately the classroom.

In our second year, we chose a district-wide rounds focus to improve the area of our poorest test score performance: mathematics. There were many factors involved in this complex problem, but one thing was clear, it was not being solved by our great financial resources. If anything, this advantage may have worked against us. As rounds work progressed, we learned that the students who had difficulty, especially in math, were being rescued from failure on a regular basis. Due to our rich resources and proximity to teaching colleges, we had two to four adults in every classroom. Any time a student became frustrated, an aide would step up to drop hints. If a student gave up, a volunteer would provide an answer. If a student got stuck, an extra person in the classroom was always there to assist. These interventions eliminated the frustration of challenge and learning that occurs from mistakes. The students were "successful" in that they completed the assignments in class and got the right answers, but the work the students actually did was in following directions, copying, answering simplified questions, and taking dictation—in short, they were primarily learning procedures without making conceptual connections or developing deeper conceptual learning of new content.

The more the network observed, the clearer it became that the performance of struggling students in the regular classroom, in special education, and in English language learners could be predicted by the low-thinking-level tasks they were doing. The next level of work involved a range of responses that included improving the coherence of instruction, coaching, curriculum, and data input. We revamped in-service for school leaders and teachers, created study groups, and involved more teachers in adaptations of rounds work at the school level. With the entire network focused on the same problem of practice, our sharing of research, strategies, and results generated real change.

Seeing Change in Student Data Reports

Student performance data subsequently rose to the top of the urban districts. Math in particular made the biggest jump, and we reset our sights on matching our results with our highest-performing suburban neighbors. The executive director of EMAC announced the end of monitoring and watch status. As he declared at a public meeting, he had never seen such progress "anywhere else in the state or in EMAC records of prior reviews." He went on to say, "The environment and culture of the Cambridge Public Schools has been transformed from a confederation of separate schools to a unified system, one that ensures [that] the needs of all children—from those with learning difficulties to those with aptitude above and beyond their grade level—are being met." In making these statements, the executive director and the EMAC report relied substantially on test scores and other measureable student performance indicators, which had risen dramatically. When a local prominent citizen wrote to the EMAC board questioning its findings, the state instituted a further review. Several months and another year of test scores later, the EMAC reasserted its findings to an even stronger degree in what must be the most extensive review ever conducted by EMAC. I cite this event because the review was external to the school district.

Instructional rounds is not a test score improvement program, and I cannot prove that rounds was the reason that school culture and student performance improved so dramatically. Nevertheless, I am quite confident that we would never have understood enough about the teaching and learning in our classrooms or realized the depth and complexity of the systemic change necessary to effect substantial improvement had we not engaged in rounds. We certainly would not have developed the common language and other strategies necessary to act as a collegial learning organization focused on shared goals. When facilitated well, instructional rounds enables a network to improve student learning at a scale that is otherwise not possible.

FINAL THOUGHTS

Real change depends on many things—not just on recommendations by a group that has done its homework. Fresh and grounded insight into specific problems is a huge beginning, but beyond this, little can happen without backing from a superintendent who recognizes the need for distributed leadership in schools across the district. Support and willingness to change practice has to be valued at the top if improvement is to be all-encompassing, enduring, and successful. In the past, the job at the top was protected by isolation. Today, such isolation no longer exists when the person at the top joins a network of equals. This is the beauty and power of rounds.

Your job as a facilitator of school improvement and your role in providing support for school and district leadership extends well beyond rounds visits. A facilitator's job more broadly is to attend to network culture by supporting the kind of organizational change necessary to implement what is learned through rounds. The focus is to help networks find ways to take responsibility for school improvement through shared leadership practice. The impact of rounds becomes evident when what is learned through rounds influences the purpose and process of budgeting, human resource allocations, job performance expectations, district and school improvement planning, and other organizational change resulting in improved teaching and learning in the classroom.

The purpose of rounds first and foremost is to improve learning at scale. This is accomplished by increasing the understanding of school and district leadership (as network members) about what good instruction looks like and how to make it happen. By improving their grasp of the instructional core as a beginning point for better understanding of teaching and learning and therefore the larger institution, network members become more effective leaders. Rounds is about developing clarity around good practice and then ensuring that the leadership and organization are there to support it. Anyone beginning the work of instructional rounds must do so with the understanding that it's a subtle but significant change in the way education and schooling are conceived and conducted and that it encompasses ongoing, evolutionary learning.

I will leave the last words to a principal of an Australian elementary school. She describes her experience of working with her colleagues in the rounds of improving learning at scale: "We have learned to have trust and confidence in what we have to offer each other. We are developing a vision for whole school/network improvement based on what is at the core of our jobs, the classroom. What is awesome is that it brings us back to why we became teachers so long ago—to help children learn."

Sample Introductory Letter for Facilitators

Dear _____:

Welcome aboard as one of X district leaders about to initiate the instructional rounds network. As facilitator for the group, I look forward to working with you.

The two-day launch session for the network is being held at X on [dates]. Our goal for the launch session is to introduce you to the context and process of instructional rounds and to provide you an opportunity to take part in a simulated rounds visit so that you will be prepared to conduct monthly rounds visits in network schools over the coming months. Each visit will demand 1½ days of your time. Network members are expected to be present for the entirety of all sessions.

We hope you will have an opportunity to read the book provided by the district, *Instructional Rounds in Education: A Network Approach to Improving Teaching and Learning*, by Elizabeth City, Richard Elmore, Sarah Fiarman, and Lee Teitel. Also see attached a brief article that summarizes the concept, which we recommend reading before the upcoming session. As you read it, please note any questions you may wish to ask.

A basic premise of this work is that improvement of student learning at scale requires the concerted effort of a network of educators such as you. While facilitators guide the instructional rounds process and support the work you will be doing, the real work of learning improvement comes from the efforts of the network members, individually and collectively. We anticipate that over the coming months, network members will assume increasing responsibility for the operation of the network and for implementing what is learned through rounds. This is why your faithful attendance is so important.

We have found the work of instructional rounds to be both fun and challenging. You will observe in classrooms, talk with students, spend many hours with colleagues in analysis, and develop recommendations to improve learning. We will continually evaluate our progress as the network assumes increasing responsibility for efficacy of professional practice in a shared culture focused upon learning improvement.

I look forward to meeting with you. Should you have questions before we meet, my email is _____, or you can reach me on my cell phone at _____.

Best wishes,

Exercise: Influences on Achievement

The following exercise is based on John Hattie's meta-analysis of more than eight hundred research studies involving over 240 million students.

OBJECTIVE

The purpose of the exercise is to increase the network participants' knowledge of research in their profession, to challenge the participants' assumptions about effective practice, and to stimulate network interest in the study of factors that affect student achievement.

BACKGROUND

Objective data and research are strategic partners to improved learning—facilitators should plan network sessions with relevant professional development segments connected to the rounds work being done. Knowledge of productive, research-proven teaching and learning practices sharpens the network members' observations and informs their analysis of, and recommendations about, what is seen in classrooms. As Hattie suggests, almost everything teachers do in classrooms helps students learn, but what we want to know is what works best.

PROCEDURE

The exercise requires two documents. List 1 shows factors that affect student learning, and list 2 shows the level of impact on student achievement for each factor, as determined by research.

The exercise is conducted as follows:

1. List 1 is distributed to each participant (seated in small groups).
2. The participants individually rate each factor on the list "high," "medium," or "low," according to their own assessment of the level of impact on student achievement for each factor. This is completed privately.
3. List 2 is distributed to the participants, who use it to privately compare the research findings with their own personal assessments recorded on the first document. List 2 groups the factors by high, medium, and low size effects, consistent with research findings.
4. The facilitator asks the participants to discuss the results with each other in small groups, sharing what they find surprising, what might be difficult to understand or accept, and what they may have an interest in pursuing.
5. After a few minutes of small-group discussion, a whole-group discussion is conducted by the facilitator. One way to begin the discussion is to ask each group to share the highlights of its discussion in light of the original questions posed by the facilitator.

LIST 1

Ability grouping, tracking, streaming	High	Medium	Low
Classroom discussion	High	Medium	Low
Cooperative vs. individualistic learning	High	Medium	Low
Coteaching and team teaching	High	Medium	Low
Direct instruction	High	Medium	Low
Drama and arts programs	High	Medium	Low
Family structure	High	Medium	Low
Feedback	High	Medium	Low
Individualized instruction	High	Medium	Low
Influence of peers	High	Medium	Low
Inquiry-based teaching	High	Medium	Low
Integrated curricula programs	High	Medium	Low
Matching teaching with learning styles	High	Medium	Low
Metacognitive strategies	High	Medium	Low
Parental involvement	High	Medium	Low
Personality	High	Medium	Low
Phonics instruction	High	Medium	Low
Principals, school leaders	High	Medium	Low
Problem-solving teaching	High	Medium	Low
Providing formative evaluation to teachers	High	Medium	Low
Questioning	High	Medium	Low
Reciprocal teaching	High	Medium	Low
Reducing class size	High	Medium	Low
Retention (holding back a year)	High	Medium	Low
Self-verbalization and self-questioning	High	Medium	Low
Student-centered teaching	High	Medium	Low
Student control over learning	High	Medium	Low
Student expectations	High	Medium	Low
Teacher clarity	High	Medium	Low
Teacher credibility in eyes of students	High	Medium	Low
Teacher expectations	High	Medium	Low
Teacher-student relationships	High	Medium	Low
Teacher subject matter knowledge	High	Medium	Low
Vocabulary programs	High	Medium	Low
Web-based learning	High	Medium	Low
Whole language	High	Medium	Low

Source: Adapted with permission from John Hattie, *Visible Learning for Teachers: Maximizing Impact on Learning* (London and New York: Routledge, 2012).

LIST 2

High Effect Size (> 0.60)

Classroom discussion	0.82
Feedback	0.75
Metacognitive strategies	0.69
Problem-solving teaching	0.61
Providing formative evaluation to teachers	0.90
Reciprocal teaching	0.74
Self-verbalization and self-questioning	0.64
Student expectations	1.44
Teacher clarity	0.75
Teacher credibility in eyes of students	0.90
Teacher-student relationships	0.72
Vocabulary programs	0.67

Medium Effect Size (0.30 to 0.60)

Cooperative vs. individualistic learning	0.59
Direct instruction	0.59
Drama and arts programs	0.35
Influence of peers	0.53
Inquiry-based teaching	0.31
Integrated curricula programs	0.39
Phonics instruction	0.54
Parental involvement	0.49
Principals, school leaders	0.39
Questioning	0.48
Student-centered teaching	0.54
Teacher expectations	0.43

Low Size Effect (< 0.30)

Ability grouping, tracking, streaming	0.12
Coteaching and team teaching	0.19
Family structure	0.18
Individualized instruction	0.22
Matching teaching with learning styles	0.17
Personality	0.18
Reducing class size	0.21

Retention (holding back a year)	−0.31
Student control over learning	0.04
Teacher subject matter knowledge	0.09
Web-based learning	0.18
Whole language	0.06

Source: Adapted with permission from John Hattie, *Visible Learning for Teachers: Maximizing Impact on Learning* (London and New York: Routledge, 2012).

Exercise: From Observation
to Evidence

Read the following observations from classroom visits. Indicate whether you would characterize each as specific (fine-grained) *and* objective (nonjudgmental).

1. Fast paced.
2. Teacher questions students about the passage they just read.
3. Students working individually even though they were in groups. Not a lot of discussion going on.
4. "Boys and girls, today's number is thirty. Who can give me a string of numbers that go up to thirty?"
5. Teachers encouraging students to think for themselves, to go deeper. High expectations for student work and student verbal responses.
6. Teacher asks, "How did you know this?" Student explains.
7. Teacher: "How are volcanoes and earthquakes similar and different?"
8. Students practicing higher-order thinking skills.
9. Lesson on the main causes of the Civil War.
10. Students made up their own questions for the read-aloud book: "Which is your favorite character?" "What do you think Gilly should do with the money?" "What do you predict will happen to Arthur?"
11. Teacher asked what clues in the story indicated impatience.
12. Too much time on discussion, not enough time on individual work.
13. Task: find different ways to create a total of 31.
    Student 1 wrote in math journal:
    $5 + 5 + 5 + 5 + 5 + 5 + 1 = 31$

$10 + 10 + 10 + 1 = 31$
Student 2:
$20 + 9 = 03$
Student 3:
$41 - 10 = 31$
$2 + 3 \times 3 + 16 = 31$

14. Excellent classroom management.
15. Teacher introduced the concept of fractions and had students apply the concept in a hands-on activity.

ANSWERS

1. No
2. No
3. Could be either; depends on problem of practice
4. Yes
5. No
6. Yes
7. Yes
8. No
9. No
10. Yes
11. Yes
12. No
13. Yes
14. No
15. No

Source: Adapted from Elizabeth A. City, Richard F. Elmore, Sarah E. Fiarman, and Lee Teitel, *Instructional Rounds in Education: A Network Approach to Improving Teaching and Learning* (Cambridge, MA: Harvard Education Press, 2009), 85.

Sources for Classroom Teaching Videos

More and more classroom teaching videos are coming on the market. I like to use some that come with the inexpensive purchase of the Facilitator's Kit for Catherine Miles Grant, Valerie L. Mills, Mary Bouck, and Ellen Davidson, *Secondary Lenses on Learning: Team Leadership for Mathematics in Middle and High Schools* (Thousand Oaks, CA: Corwin Press, 2009). The CD in the Facilitator's Kit includes several exemplary lessons of uninterrupted classroom action with minimal editing.

Another good, free source of typical middle school math and science teaching can be obtained at the web site http://timssvideo.com. These videos from the Trends in International Mathematics and Science Study come with minimal editing, show uninterrupted action, are accompanied by transcripts, and can be downloaded at no cost. There are four math lessons from seven countries and five science lessons from five countries. These videos are more than ten years old.

The most exhaustive source of free videos demonstrating exemplary teaching in all subject areas and all grades can be obtained from Annenberg Media. Its mission is to disseminate best practices to teachers in K–12. These videos have voice-overs of teachers explaining what they are doing and why. When I use the videos, I mute the voice-over portions so that the participants taking observation notes can concentrate objectively on the live action in the classroom. The videos are free for school use and can be found at the Annenberg Learner web site, www.learner.org/index.html. (CD versions of the videos, or permission to download the videos can be purchased.)

Delta/Plus Feedback Protocol

The delta/plus feedback protocol helps the network members take responsibility for their own learning by providing feedback to the facilitator at the conclusion of the network's first day together. The facilitator learns what the participants found helpful and what may require adjustment or may need to be added on the second day to improve the participant learning experience. The members respond to the three questions listed below. Ask the participants to write every individual response on a separate sticky note, using as many sticky notes as they wish. The participants then paste their notes on the appropriate poster boards labeled "Plus," "Changes," and "?" as they leave the session. Facilitators present the results of the feedback to the network at the beginning of the next day.

- What's one thing that helped your learning today? (Paste answers on the "Plus" page.)
- What's one change we could make that would help your learning? (Paste on the "Changes" page.)
- What lingering questions do you have? (Paste on the "?" page.)

The Instructional Core Analysis Framework

Action Trajectories for Teacher and Student

OVERVIEW OF SHIFT OVER LEVELS 0 TO 3

The classroom community grows to support students acting in central or leading roles and shifts from a focus on answers to a focus on subject matter thinking.

A. Questioning	B. Explaining Content Thinking	C. Source of Content Ideas	D. Responsibility for Learning
Shift from teacher as questioner to students and teacher as questioners.	Students increasingly explain and articulate their content ideas.	Shift from teacher as the source of all content ideas to students' ideas also influencing the direction of the lesson.	Students increasingly take responsibility for learning and the evaluation of others and self. Content sense becomes the criterion for evaluation.

LEVEL 0

Traditional teacher-directed classroom with brief answer responses from students.

A. Questioning	B. Explaining Content Thinking	C. Source of Content Ideas	D. Responsibility for Learning
Teacher is the only questioner. Short, frequent questions function to keep students listening and paying attention to the teacher. Students give short answers and respond to the teacher only. No student-to-student content talk.	No or minimal teacher elicitation of student thinking, strategies, or explanations; teacher expects answer-focused responses. Teacher may tell answers. No student thinking or strategy-focused explanation of work. Only answers are given.	Teacher is physically at the front, usually telling and showing students how to do the work. Students respond to work presented by the teacher. They do not offer their own content ideas.	Teacher repeats student responses (originally directed to her) for the class. Teacher responds to students' answers by verifying the correct answer or showing the correct method. Students are passive listeners; they attempt to imitate the teacher and do not take responsibility for the learning of their peers or themselves.

LEVEL 1

Teacher is beginning to pursue student subject matter thinking. Teacher plays central role in the content-talk community.

A. Questioning	B. Explaining Content Thinking	C. Source of Content Ideas	D. Responsibility for Learning
Teacher questions begin to focus on student thinking and focus less on answers. Teacher begins to ask follow-up questions about student methods.	Teacher probes student thinking somewhat. One or two strategies may be elicited. Teacher may fill in explanations herself.	Teacher is still the main source of ideas, though she or he elicits some student ideas. Teacher does some probing to access student ideas.	Teacher begins to set up structures to facilitate students' listening to and helping other students. The teacher alone gives feedback.
As a student answers a question, other students listen passively or wait for their turn.	Students give information about their content thinking usually as it is probed by the teacher (minimal volunteering of thoughts). They provide brief descriptions of their thinking.	Some student ideas are raised in discussions, but are not explored.	Students become more engaged by repeating what other students say or by helping another student at the teacher's request. This helping mostly involves students' showing how they did their work.

LEVEL 2

Teacher is modeling and helping students build new roles. Some coteaching and colearning begin as student-to-student talk increases. Teacher physically begins to move to side or back of the room.

A. Questioning	B. Explaining Content Thinking	C. Source of Content Ideas	D. Responsibility for Learning
Teacher continues to ask probing questions and asks more-open questions. She or he also facilitates student-to-student talk, e.g., by asking students to be prepared to ask questions about other students' work.	Teacher probes more deeply to learn about student thinking and supports detailed descriptions from students. Teacher open to and elicits multiple strategies.	Teacher follows up on explanations and builds on them by asking students to compare and contrast them. Teacher is comfortable using student errors as opportunities for learning.	Teacher encourages student responsibility for understanding the content ideas of others. Teacher asks other students questions about student work and whether they agree or disagree and why.
Students ask questions of one another's work, often at the prompting of the teacher. Students listen to one another so they do not repeat questions.	Students usually give information as it is probed by the teacher, with some volunteering of thoughts. They begin to stake a position and articulate more information in response to probes. They explain steps in their thinking by providing fuller descriptions and begin to defend their answers and methods. Other students listen supportively.	Students exhibit confidence about their ideas and share their own thinking and strategies even if the ideas are different from others' ideas. Student ideas sometimes guide the direction of the lesson.	Students begin to listen to understand one another. When the teacher requests, they explain other students' ideas in their own words. Helping involves clarifying other students' ideas for themselves and others. Students imitate and model teacher's probing in pair work and in whole-class discussions.

LEVEL 3

Teacher acts as coteacher and colearner. Teacher monitors all that occurs, still fully engaged. Teacher is ready to assist, but now in more peripheral and monitoring role (coach and assister).

A. Questioning	B. Explaining Content Thinking	C. Source of Content Ideas	D. Responsibility for Learning
Teacher expects students to ask one another questions about their work. The teacher's questions still may guide the discourse. Student-to-student talk is student-initiated, not dependent on the teacher. Students ask questions and listen to responses. Many questions are why questions that require justification from the person answering. Students repeat their own or others' questions until satisfied with answers.	Teacher follows along closely to student descriptions of their thinking, encouraging students to make their explanations more compete; may ask probing questions to make explanations more complete. Teacher stimulates students to think more deeply about strategies. Students describe more complete strategies; they defend and justify their answers with little prompting from the teacher. Students realize that they will be asked questions from other students when they finish, so they are motivated and careful to be thorough. Other students support with active listening.	Teacher allows for interruptions from students during her explanations; he or she lets students explain and own the new strategies. (Teacher is still engaged and deciding what is important to continue exploring.) Teacher uses student ideas and methods as the basis for lessons or mini-extensions. Students interject their ideas as the teacher or other students are teaching, confident that their ideas are valued. Students spontaneously compare and contrast and build on ideas. Student ideas form part of the content of many lessons.	The teacher expects students to be responsible for coevaluation of everyone's work and thinking. She or he supports students as they help one another sort out misconceptions. Teacher helps and follows up when needed. Students listen to understand, and then initiate clarifying other students' work and ideas for themselves and for others during whole-class discussions as well as in small-group and pair work. Students assist each other in understanding and correcting errors.

Source: Adapted with permission from *Journal for Research in Mathematics Education.* Copyright © 2004 by the National Council of Teachers of Mathematics. All rights reserved.

ACKNOWLEDGMENTS

Sometimes, profound ideas come your way and enable you to understand more clearly something you thought you already knew completely, causing you to think, why didn't I see it before?

This is what I experienced in my first encounter with instructional rounds and the Harvard team of Richard Elmore, Elizabeth City, and Sarah Fiarman. They were brilliant in guiding our school district's Cambridge Leadership Network. They helped us learn far more than we ever anticipated through teaching us to work ever more powerfully and cooperatively to advance our professional practice and therefore the learning of our Cambridge students. I am greatly indebted to them for that start to a more productive career, as well as for their continued counsel, open exchange of ideas, and friendship.

I remain impressed with the ongoing work of the Cambridge network, particularly that of Cambridge Schools Deputy Superintendent Carolyn Turk, who, at my urging, assumed the role of facilitator once our work with the Harvard team was complete. I have learned a tremendous amount from watching and working with her as well as from my other network colleagues about implementing what we learned from rounds.

My professional growth in this area is indebted to a number of other exceptional educators and colleagues who have shared this journey with me—raising questions, finding ways to move the work forward, and trying a variety of approaches—all of which have led me to make adjustments to my own rounds practice. Many people come to mind, but of special note are those with whom I have worked over several years; all of them are passionate about improving student learning: Karen Cain of the Gippsland Region schools, who got me started as a facilitator in her district and whose dedication to adult and student learning is an inspiration; Michonne Van Rees in Gippsland and Katherine Henderson and Terry Lawless in the Western Metropolitan Region network, who, along with many regional network leaders, boldly took on the work, and made suggestions that have found their way into the pages of this book; and Lee Teitel, another member of the Harvard team, whose thoughtful remarks in the foreword of the book continue to enrich my understanding of facilitation experiences.

Rachel Goldberg in New Jersey offered her enthusiastic support and terrific suggestions about what would be helpful to those taking on the work of rounds facilitation, while her boss, Pablo Munoz, sets so high a bar, his rounds work has always challenged me to improve, particularly in the difficult follow-up work.

Writing a book like this is daunting. Trying to simplify a subject that by its very nature is subtle and complex has been enormously difficult. For this reason, I am fortunate to have benefited from the intelligent insights, supportive advice, and continuous encouragement of Harvard Education Press editor Caroline Chauncey as well as editorial assistance from award-winning journalist Colleen Gillard. Colleen not only is a bright and talented writer, but has earned my respect and gratitude for persevering—with such good humor—through the long, intense months of this project.

Last, and most of all, I need to thank the love of my life, my wife Sue, who innocently and bravely gave up the dining room, the living room, and then still more space to the book, even as contractors were tearing out our bedroom. Her encouragement and support have been tremendous.

ABOUT THE AUTHOR

Thomas Fowler-Finn, founder of Instructional Rounds Plus, works as a consultant nationally and internationally to improve leadership practices in education through instructional rounds. He has dedicated his professional life as a teacher, principal, and superintendent to the belief that all students deserve better. In this pursuit, he has turned around urban and suburban school districts, receiving multiple honors and awards.

During his tenure as superintendent of the Cambridge Public Schools, the district was honored as one of the most improved school systems in the state by the Educational Quality and Accountability agency of the governor's office. As superintendent of the 32,000-student Fort Wayne urban school district, Tom was honored by Governor Frank O'Bannon with the highest citizen leadership honor awarded by the state of Indiana. Other distinctions include twice being honored by the Massachusetts State Department of Education for exceptional leadership and vision, selection as a model of school corporation success by the International Centre for Leadership in Education and by the National School Board Association, and identification by the Wallace Foundation as being among the top school superintendents in the nation.

Additional open-source resources for facilitators are available at www.instructional rounds.com or by contacting the author at tfowlerfin@gmail.com.

INDEX

inconsistent with stated focus of lesson
pattern, 147
teachers
ascribing motive to actions, 141
blaming for poor student performance,
45
called on students with hands raised
pattern, 145–146
conceptual problems, 143
dependency on, 141
describing comments of, 141
doing work for students, 149
engaging in instructional rounds,
185–186
excluding from rounds visits, 39–40
expectations, 149
expecting rounds visits, 39–40
gradual release of responsibility, 62
informing about instructional rounds,
35
interaction with students in presence
of content, 3, 51, 60
misinterpreting checking for
understanding, 141
misunderstanding praise by, 140–141
observation used to judge and evaluate,
51
patterns focusing too much on, 139
problems of practice, 45–46
protocols of classroom observations,
94
providing with visit schedule, 40
questions at recall or understanding
level pattern, 146–147
role of, 36, 62
volunteers for observation, 39
teacher-student interactions, 111–112
teacher-student roles, 95

teaching
best practices, 52–53
district-wide high-quality, 5
evidence supporting predictions, 151
observing around problems, 36
shared understanding of effective, 3
systemic improvement, 5
typical situations, 70
teaching practices
cause and effect of, 112
videos modeling, 68–69
teams
balancing size and networks, 25–26
cognitive demand between assignment
and completion of task, 142
finishing at different times, 142
initial debriefing of observations, 25
patterns, 142, 145
predictions, 151
screening protocol for evidence, 88
strategic starting points, 166–167
struggling with screening decisions,
128
table facilitators, 127–128
working too slowly, 127–128
team screening protocol
common problems and solutions,
127–129
identical notes, 126
multiple perspectives, 126
organizing evidence, 128–129
patterns, 129–130
pooling data, 129–133
problems with pooling evidence,
129–130
reading sticky notes out loud, 125
red-dot protocol, 130–133
reviewing evidence, 125–127